Corporations and Partnerships in Brazil

Corporations and Partnerships in Brazil

Third Edition

Eduardo Salomão Neto

Jorge Eduardo Prada Levy

Isabela Schenberg Frascino

This book was originally published as a monograph in the International Encyclopaedia of Laws/Corporations and Partnerships.

Founding Editor: Roger Blanpain
General Editor: Frank Hendrickx
Volume Editor: Sofie Cools

Wolters Kluwer

Published by:
Kluwer Law International B.V.
PO Box 316
2400 AH Alphen aan den Rijn
The Netherlands
E-mail: lrs-sales@wolterskluwer.com
Website: www.wolterskluwer.com/en/solutions/kluwerlawinternational

Sold and distributed by:
Wolters Kluwer Legal & Regulatory U.S.
920 Links Avenue
Landisville, PA 17538
United States of America
E-mail: customer.service@wolterskluwer.com

Printed on acid-free paper

ISBN 978-94-035-2019-3

e-Book: ISBN 978-94-035-2029-2
web-PDF: ISBN 978-94-035-2039-1

The Authors

Eduardo Salomão Neto is a partner at the Brazilian law firm Levy & Salomão Advogados, based in São Paulo. He graduated in Law from the Faculty of Laws at the University of São Paulo in 1985 and obtained an LLM in Commercial Law and Taxation from the University of London in 1987. He also has a PhD and a post-doctorate degree in Commercial Law from the Faculty of Laws at the University of São Paulo.

He is the author of O Trust e o Direito Brasileiro (The Trust and Brazilian Law), São Paulo, Trevisan, 2016, Direito Bancário (Banking Law), São Paulo, Atlas, 2020 and several articles on commercial and tax law.

Jorge Eduardo Prada Levy is a partner at the Brazilian law firm Levy & Salomão Advogados, based in São Paulo. He graduated in law at the Faculty of Laws of the University of São Paulo in 1986. He has also worked as a member of the legal department of the São Paulo Stock Exchange (1986–1987) and was president of the Brazilian Bank Association ABBC (2001–2002).

The Authors

Isabela Schenberg Frascino is a partner at the Brazilian law firm Levy & Salomão Advogados, based in São Paulo. She focuses on tax planning and complex transactions, often involving multinational corporations and their subsidiaries. Ms Frascino holds an LLM from Harvard University, Cambridge, Massachusetts.

Table of Contents

List of Abbreviations

BCA	Lei das Sociedades Anônimas (Brazilian Corporations Act). Corporations in Brazil are regulated by Law No. 6404, dated 15 December 1976, with substantial amendments introduced by Law No. 10303, dated 31 October 2001
BCC	Código Civil Brasileiro (Brazilian Civil Code). The Brazilian Civil Code currently in force was enacted by Law No. 10406, dated 10 January 2002. Until this date, the Brazilian private legal system has been regulated by the Civil Code (1916) and the Commercial Code (1850). The new Brazilian Civil Code unified both commercial and civil rules and introduced several important modifications to the Brazilian legal system
CMN	Conselho Monetário Nacional (National Monetary Council). The CMN is a federal entity created by Law No. 4595, dated 31 December 1964, for the purpose of defining the national policy as to currency and credit in accordance with the directives established by the President of the Republic
COFINS	Contribuição para o Financiamento da Seguridade Social (Contribution for the Financing of Social Security). COFINS was established by Complementary Law No. 70, dated 30 December 1991
CSLL	Contribuição Social sobre o Lucro Líquido (Social Contribution on Net Profit). CSLL was created by Law No. 7689, dated 15 December 1988
CSRF	Superior Court of Administrative Tax Appeals
CVM	Comissão de Valores Mobiliários (Securities Commission). The CVM is the federal regulatory agency created by Law No. 6385, dated 7 December 1976, which is responsible for the regulation and supervision of the securities market
DREI	Department of Commerce Registration and Integration
INE	Interest on Net Equity (Juros sobre o Capital Próprio)
IRPJ	Corporate Income Tax (Imposto de Renda da Pessoa Jurídica)

List of Abbreviations

PIS	Contribuição para o Programa de Integração Social (Social Integration Program). PIS was created by Complementary Law No. 7, dated 7 September 1970
TP	Transfer Pricing (preços de transferência)
WHT	Withholding Income Tax (Imposto de Renda Retido na Fonte)

Preface

Brazil's corporate law framework is influenced by both its civil law tradition and modern global practices, creating a unique legal landscape. This preface aims to provide a foundational overview of the principles and practices that underpin corporate law in Brazil, highlighting its significance and the ongoing developments that shape its application.

The text begins by delving into the broader context of the country, encompassing its geography, cultural composition and political system and their correlation with key economic indicators. The structure of a developing country turns out to be receptive to investment and new business.

After presenting the country's general scenario, the authors deal concisely with the origins and historical evolution of Brazilian companies, briefly tracing the legislative roots and the evolution of corporate law.

Since understanding Brazilian commercial law is essential for anyone engaged in business within the country, whether they are investors, entrepreneurs, multinational corporations, or legal professionals, the text focuses on and describes the legal structure of Brazilian corporations and companies.

The authors elucidate the distinctions between various business entities and operations, such as mergers, consolidations, and spin-offs that exist in Brazil. Among other topics covered are the nuances of single-shareholder companies, the incorporation processes for limited liability companies and corporations, the formation of share capital, formal aspects of shareholders' meetings, matters relating to administration, the liabilities and rights of directors and of the shareholders themselves.

The text also addresses pivotal elements of labour law, including the implications of legal entities disregarded by labour courts and relevant aspects of Brazilian tax law, such as the different taxes applicable to legal entities in Brazil.

General Introduction

§1. General Background of the Country

I. Geography

1. The Federative Republic of Brazil occupies two-thirds of South America (3,286,473 square miles) and is one of the largest countries in the world, smaller only than Russia, Canada, China, and the United States (US). Brazil's climate is very diversified, mainly tropical and subtropical, with average temperatures ranging from around 40 degrees Centigrade (109°F) in the northeast to 20 degrees Centigrade (68°F) in the southeast and even to below 0 degrees Centigrade (32°F) in the deep south, during winter. Climate variety coupled with soil fertility makes Brazil a potentially productive area where varied crops may be grown.

Brazil's territorial area supplies mineral resources on a large scale, for instance, iron ore (estimated reserves: 76 billion tons), bauxite (2.7 billion tons),[1] potassium (14.4 billion tons), copper (11.2 million tons),[2] and manganese (272 million tons).[3] *Serra dos Carajás*, one of Brazil's largest reserves, contains about 18 billion tons of high iron content ore and 50 million tons of manganese, besides significant quantities of copper, nickel, chromium, tin, and gold.[4] The country is irrigated by a large basin of rivers that furnish hydraulic power, which represents the main generating capacity for this sort of energy, followed by coal, charcoal, and natural gas plants. Other energy sources are minimal, such as nuclear and wind energy, among others.[5]

1. SUMÁRIO MINERAL 2018, Agência Nacional de Mineração, in https://www.gov.br/anm/pt-br/centrais-de-conteudo/publicacoes/serie-estatisticas-e-economia-mineral/sumario-mineral/sumario-mineral-brasileiro-2018 (last accessed on 20 Oct. 2023).
2. SUMÁRIO MINERAL 2017, Agência Nacional de Mineração, in https://www.gov.br/anm/pt-br/centrais-de-conteudo/publicacoes/serie-estatisticas-e-economia-mineral/sumario-mineral/sumariomineral_2017 (last accessed on 20 Oct. 2023).
3. SUMÁRIO MINERAL 2018, Agência Nacional de Mineração, in https://www.gov.br/anm/pt-br/centrais-de-conteudo/publicacoes/serie-estatisticas-e-economia-mineral/sumario-mineral/sumario-mineral-brasileiro-2018 (last accessed on 20 Oct. 2023).
4. CPRM – Serviço Geológico Brasil, in http://www.cprm.gov.br/publique/media/informacao_publica/rel_anual_2015.pdf (last accessed on 23 Oct. 2023). p. 4.
5. Ministério de Minas e Energia – Relatório anual 2015 http://www.aben.com.br/Arquivos/456/456.pdf (last accessed 23 Oct. 2023).

II. Cultural Composition

2. Brazil was colonized by the Portuguese, and this fact resulted in a strong influence on European patterns. Such influence has been increased by the flow of European immigrants (mostly Italians and Germans) towards the southern region of the country in the nineteenth century and the beginning of the twentieth century.

The influence of African culture should also be mentioned, since both before and after independence (1822), many slaves were brought to the country from Africa to work in agriculture. As for the native indigenous population, its cultural influence is mainly to be felt in the northern region of the country, where the influence of colonization was more tenuous. Many natural reserves for indigenous populations are maintained by the government.

III. Political System

3. The country is a federated republic of twenty-six states and one federal district. Executive power is exercised by the president, who remains in office for a four-year term, aided by the ministers of state. The Legislature is composed of a bicameral National Congress consisting of the Federal Senate and the Chamber of Representatives. In November 1989, presidential elections through direct voting were held in the country for the first time after twenty-one years of the dictatorial-militarist system.

The vote is mandatory after the age of 18 and optional between 16 and 18 and after 60. It is also optional for the illiterate. The formation, spin-off, and merger of political parties are free (Federal Constitution, Article 17), with the existence of several officially recognized political parties.

IV. Population and Employment Statistics

4. Like other developing countries, Brazil is experiencing demographic growth, with a population of about 203 million people (in 2022). Statistics show a trend towards a substantial decrease in population growth. One of the main consequences arising from this is that the Brazilian population is mainly composed of adults, the age group over 30 years old now accounts for more than 56.1% of the population.[6] This population, increasing at the average annual rate of 0.52%, accounts for a quite inexpensive but non-specialized labour force, besides portraying a continuously expanding potential market. Preliminary data of 2022 shows that 61% of the

6. Agência IBGE – https://agenciadenoticias.ibge.gov.br/agencia-noticias/2012-agencia-de-noticias/noticias/34438-populacao-cresce-mas-numero-de-pessoas-com-menos-de-30-anos-cai-5-4-de-2012-a-2021 (last accessed on 7 Nov. 2023).

population (124.1 million people) dwells in urban areas.[7] Brazil also has a high number of European and Japanese immigrants.

V. Enterprise and Corporations/Partnerships Statistics

5. During the year 2022, 3,838,063 new business ventures were initiated throughout the country.[8] It should be pointed out that most enterprises created in this period were incorporated as 'micro-enterprises', thus qualifying to obtain tax reductions (Complementary Law No. 123, dated 14 December 2006).

In 2022, from a total of 20,191,290 formal business ventures existing in the country by the end of the year, 57.6% were individual unincorporated enterprises (individual micro-entrepreneurs), and 29.4% were limited liability companies.

Together, about 87% of the business ventures in Brazil bear one of these forms. The other types of business associations admitted by Brazilian Commercial Law, including corporations, represent only roughly 13%.

The ventures were formed mainly in the southeast, about 1,927,891, where the economic centre of the country is located.[9] The average time for opening businesses in the country is one day.

Among the economic sectors, the services sector was distinguished by the highest concentration of initiation of new business ventures (about 49.6%), followed by the retail business (about 31.9%) and industry (about 9.1%).[10]

Individual unincorporated enterprises represent the majority of the newly begun ventures (74.7%) in the last quarter of 2022, followed by limited liability companies (20.8%).

VI. Social and Cultural Values

6. Brazil has typical social characteristics of developing countries. This is linked to the existence of large cities – especially in the southern region – strongly marked by modern and foreign influences, alongside backward inland regions, where the permanence of an agricultural economic structure tends to favour conservatism and illiteracy.

---

7. Educa IBGE in https://educa.ibge.gov.br/jovens/materias-especiais/21972-populacao-brasileira-cresce-6-5-e-chega-a-203-1-milhoes-de-habitantes-aponta-censo-2022.html (last accessed on 20 Oct. 2023).
8. Ministério da Economia, in https://www.gov.br/economia/pt-br/assuntos/noticias/2023/janeiro/brasil-registrou-abertura-de-3-838-063-novas-empresas-em-2022 (last accessed on 23 Oct. 2023).
9. Mapa de Empresas – Boletim do 3° Quadrimestre de 2022 in https://www.gov.br/empresas-e-negocios/pt-br/mapa-de-empresas/boletins/mapa-de-empresas-boletim-3o-quadrimestre-2022.pdf (last accessed on 23 Oct. 2023).
10. Mapa de Empresas – Boletim do 3° Quadrimestre de 2022 in https://www.gov.br/empresas-e-negociospt-br/mapa-de-empresas/boletins/mapa-de-empresas-boletim-3o-quadrimestre-2022.pdf (last accessed on 23 Oct. 2023).

Brazil is a traditionally tolerant country in relation to religion. The religion prevailing in the country is Catholicism, but any kind of worship may be freely adopted.

§2. Historical Background of Corporations and Partnerships

I. General Considerations: Partnerships

7. In Brazil, the legal regulation of partnerships preceded the legal regulation of limited liability companies and corporations. Brazilian partnerships, based on contract, can be traced to their Roman-law origins. In fact, their most remote form in Roman law was the joint ownership kept by the heirs in relation to the inherited estate, a legal structure then called *erctus non citus.* From this, the concept developed to become one of the basic Roman consensual contracts then called *societas.* Such concept, after being relatively neglected during the Middle Ages, found its rebirth in the classical studies made during the Renaissance and influenced the period of codification through which civil-law systems went after the French Revolution. Through this rebirth, the concept found its way into Portuguese law and subsequently into the law of former Portuguese territories, as has been the case with Brazil, since independence in 1822.

Partnerships first received codification in the country in the Brazilian Commercial Code. Such Code was prepared to provide Brazil with its own legislation in commercial matters, since Portuguese laws had been provisionally kept in force in the country with a supplementary character since independence. The Code's first part, which regulated commerce in general, was revoked by the Brazilian Civil Code (BCC) in 2002, but its remaining provisions, which regulate sea trade, are still in force.

II. Limited Liability Companies

8. Brazilian limited liability companies, the *sociedade limitada,* can also be traced to their foreign origins. They appeared in foreign legal systems as a consequence of the trend for limitation of liability that came with the industrial revolution and the development of capitalism. Their origins date from a German law on limited liability companies that came into force on 20 April 1892, which was subsequently copied by Portugal in 1901. In Brazil, an attempt was made in 1865 to introduce a simplified form of share company with limited liability based on French and English initiatives. The project was not successful. Later, based on the successful German and Portuguese experiences, a project on limited liability companies, providing them with a legal regime different from that of share companies, was prepared by Herculano Inglez de Souza, a Brazilian legal scholar. This project was transformed into Decree No. 3708, dated 10 January 1919. Up to the enactment of the BCC, which has been in force since 10 January 2003 that was the only statute that specifically regulated limited liability companies. The BCC extensively regulates such companies and partnerships.

III. Corporations

9. As to the origin of corporations, there are many possibilities that can be taken into account. In Rome, a kind of limited liability corporation was formed by parties acquiring from the state the right to charge taxes in colonial territories, being called *societas publicanorum.* In the Renaissance, banks and transnational enterprises (such as the Medici group) originating from the Italian republics were said to bear the form of corporations, a still much-debated point. Finally, the colonial companies incorporated through the granting of Royal Charters for the exploitation of colonial ventures can also be compared to corporations. Such companies were used as instruments for financing expansion overseas and embodied state and private capital.

Further on, in the nineteenth century, corporations as a legal form became the answer to a very important trend of capitalism as it developed from the industrial revolution: the need to limit liability and provide means for the concentration of capital in the hands of an organism able to invest it in business activities in the most professional and profitable way. As an answer to such needs, corporations were freed from most barriers to their incorporation. Such barriers had been imposed in the aftermath of the French Revolution in order to abolish corporatism and medieval privileges; an example was the need to obtain a Royal Charter or government authorization prior to incorporation. In Brazil, the tendency towards liberalization was present during the nineteenth century. Corporations were statutorily regulated by the Brazilian Commercial Code of 1850, which, in Article 295, followed the prevailing trend and made them dependent on governmental authorization in any circumstances. This was revoked, and the corporations were freed from any limits regarding their incorporation through Decree No. 8821, dated 30 December 1882. Due to a severe crisis provoked by speculation, the Brazilian Commercial Code had several provisions relating to corporations modified and others codified by Decree No. 434, dated 4 July 1891.

Finally, the Brazilian Commercial Code provisions relating to corporations were revoked by Decree Law No. 2627, issued on 26 September 1940. This statute was based upon a project by the legal scholar Trajano de Miranda Valverde that provided a fairly technical and sophisticated framework for the period. The needs at that time required a corporation form to be able to accommodate the complex administrative structures typical of the large businesses that had by then already developed. Reforms to Decree Law No. 2627/40 were introduced in the mid-sixties with the intent of developing Brazilian capital markets and broadening capital ownership through Law No. 4728, dated 14 July 1965, and through the administrative regulations organizing the stock exchanges. These changes partially answered new imperatives brought by the swift period of economic and entrepreneurial development undergone by Brazil in the sixties and seventies with the arrival in the country of large multinational groups.

However, the legal rules relating to corporations still needed development, especially in order to strengthen the position of minority shareholders. This had been, to a certain extent, neglected until then since Decree Law No. 2627/40 was enacted at a time in which most businesses were family-owned. For the purpose of accommodating those needs, the government put together, at the beginning of the seventies, a commission of legal experts in order to prepare a project of a new statute on corporations. The project was transformed into Law No. 6404, enacted on 15 December 1976 as the Brazilian Corporations Act (BCA). Such statute, in accordance with the reasons that motivated its creation, provided specific rules for the imposition of liability on controlling shareholders and broadened the rights of the minority (including the right to a minimum dividend). Besides, it also had the aim of boosting the concentration of capital in large business concerns, thus providing detailed regulation on groups of companies, mergers, spin-offs, and acquisitions. Technically, the new statute was much influenced by the common-law model, especially the American one. It is thus reflected in several topics (duties of officers, duties of controlling shareholders, agent for the debenture holders), as well as the fiduciary duties and trust concepts that permeate company law as developed in England and the US.

Law No. 6404 is still the basis of Brazilian corporations' regulation; however, it has been amended by several later statutes. It is worth mentioning Law No. 9457, dated 5 May 1997, which mainly altered the rules regarding transfer of control of publicly held corporations in order to enable the government to proceed with privatization in the telecommunications sector. Further, on 31 October 2001, Law No. 10303 came into force and introduced substantial amendments to Law No. 6404. Among others, it is worth mentioning rules regarding the proportion of preferential shares, duty to inform, and election of the Board of Directors. References to the BCA in this text will include the changes implemented by all later statutes that amended Law No. 6404, including Law No. 9457 and Law No. 10303. Law No. 11638, dated 28 December 2007, changed certain accounting rules in order to bring Brazilian accounting closer to international accounting standards. More recently, there have been changes brought by Law No. 14195, dated 26 August 2021, commonly referred to as the Business Environment Law, which aimed to improve the business environment in Brazil and introduced reforms to the BCA, including, for example, the super voting shares, as explained below. It is also worth mentioning Complementary Law No. 182, dated 1 June 2021, the Startup Legal Framework, which sought to create favourable conditions for smaller corporations to access the capital market.

No historical account of the law of business associations in Brazil will be complete if it is not recognized that legal development has preceded economic development in the subject. As an example of this, the first corporation whose control was traded in the securities market appeared only in 2005. Also, it is worth noting that from April 2004 until July 2024, a total of 528 public offers of shares took place in Brazilian capital markets, including both IPOs and FOLLOW-ONs.[11] The boom of public offerings in 2020 and 2021 did not change the fact that family-type businesses, even if of substantial size, still prevail in the country.

11. Information available at B3 website https://www.b3.com.br/pt_br/produtos-e-servicos/solucoes-para-emissores/ofertas-publicas/estatisticas/ (last accessed on 23 Oct. 2023).

§3. Definitions and Structure of Corporations and Partnerships

I. The Distinction Between Corporations, Limited Liability Companies, and Partnerships in Brazil

10. The first major difficulty to be dealt with in relation to the distinction between the corporate forms is finding a suitable criterion to set apart corporations and limited liability companies from partnerships.

Some possible criteria that might be adopted elsewhere are the existence of legal personality, limited liability and the absence of a contractual relationship between the members of corporations, whereas the contrary would apply to partnerships. Such rules of thumb, however, do not apply in Brazil. In fact, according to Article 44 of the BCC, all corporations, limited liability companies, and partnerships (except for partnerships upon settlement) are granted legal personality. Limited liability does not represent a safe criterion for separating corporations and limited liability companies from partnerships. In fact, whereas it is indeed present in the former categories, Brazilian law also admits, as will be seen, several forms of partnerships with limited liability partners. As for the absence of a contractual relationship, it could not be the grounds for a successful distinction since Brazilian legal doctrine sustains the existence of a contractual relationship among the members of limited liability companies and also among the members of privately held corporations and partnerships. Besides, the existence of a contractual relationship between the members of a limited liability company and between the members of partnerships is affirmed beyond doubt by Articles 1001–1009 of the BCC, which establish rights and obligations for any member of such associations.

The real criterion for affecting the distinction seems to be grounded in the fact that business associations typically group persons or capital, whereas partnerships are typically designed to join persons. Such assertion is proven by the fact that the personal contribution of the partners is fundamental for the development of the activities of the partnership. Accordingly, the partners to a partnership (or at least one of them) are prevented from transferring their interest to third parties without the unanimous agreement of all the other partners, as set forth in Articles 997 and 999 of the BCC. In view of the personal character of the partnership, the partners are also prevented from pledging their shares. Similar rules apply to limited liability companies, in which the partners are free to transfer their interests to other partners – if there is no rule to the contrary in the articles of incorporation – but a transfer to third parties is only possible if there is no opposition from company members representing more than 25% of the capital stock, as set forth in Article 1057 of the BCC. Conversely, it can be said that corporations are typically incorporated for joining capital, having as characteristics free circulation of shares and the continuation of their existence regardless of personal circumstances affecting their members, such as insolvency or death.

In view of the above, we will be handling corporations and limited liability companies in Part I below, as well as all sorts of partnerships (simple partnerships, unlimited partnerships, limited partnerships, limited partnerships by shares, and partnerships upon settlement) in Part II.

II. The Distinction Between Corporations and Limited Liability Companies

11. In Part I, it will be necessary to distinguish between corporations and limited liability companies. In Brazil, this is a question of fact rather than a question of law. Since corporations present extensive disclosure and public-notice requirements relating to their meetings and financial statements, which can be costly, such legal form tends to be typical of larger concerns. Besides, only corporations may have their capital or debentures traded on the stock exchanges and stock markets according to Article 2 of Law No. 6385, dated 7 December 1976. Thus, all publicly traded companies are presently corporations. Conversely, most small businesses tend to be formed as limited liability companies in order to trade under the cover of limited liability while enjoying a relatively simple legal framework. However, the law does not prevent limited liability companies from carrying on extensive trade or business, nor does it restrict the number of their quota holders. In fact, there are several instances in which large business ventures are conducted under the form of a limited liability company, which may be for such purpose contractually endowed with a rather complex administrative structure, similar to that of a corporation, without losing its character. It should be noted that large limited liability companies are required to follow the accounting rules applicable to corporations and have their accounts examined by independent auditors (Article 3 of Law No. 11638/07). A limited liability company is deemed to be large if it has assets higher than BRL 240 million or annual gross revenues exceeding BRL 300 million (Article 3 of Law No. 11638/07).

III. The Question of the Entrepreneurial Nature of Companies

12. Brazilian law makes a distinction between entrepreneurial and non-entrepreneurial companies. Article 966 of the BCC considers entrepreneurs as those who professionally perform economic activities organized for the production or circulation of goods or services. Its sole paragraph states that those who develop activities of an intellectual, scientific, literary, or artistic nature, even if with the assistance of third parties, will not be deemed as entrepreneurs, provided that the production means are not professionally organized. Thus, the difference lies in the manner through which the company pursues its corporate goal. The vast majority of companies incorporated in Brazil are of an entrepreneurial nature.

As to the law of business associations, the main consequence of the dichotomy between entrepreneurial and non-entrepreneurial associations is the obligation to register the former with the Commercial Registrar of Legal Entities, whereas the latter have their constituting documents filed with the Civil Registrar. Other practical consequences can be noted regarding the differences between entrepreneurial and non-entrepreneurial companies:

- entrepreneurial companies may be subject to bankruptcy and composition with creditors as per Law No. 11101, dated 9 February 2005, conducted by specialized court divisions in the largest cities, whereas non-entrepreneurial companies are subject to simplified insolvency proceedings conducted by non-specialized court divisions, under the terms of Articles 748 and following of the Brazilian Civil Procedure Code of 1973, still in force besides the enactment of the new Brazilian Civil Procedure Code of 2015; and

- partnerships, limited liability companies and corporations bearing an entrepreneurial character may plea before the courts to have any leases of buildings used for commerce or industry for the last five years extended for a period equal to that of the original agreement, regardless of the acquiescence of the landlord, in terms of Law No. 8245, dated 18 October 1991 – a right that is, as a general rule, not extended to business associations bearing a non-entrepreneurial character.

IV. Non-profit/Non-corporate Associations

13. This introduction would not be complete without a reference to the rules applicable to non-profit and non-corporate entities under Brazilian law. Brazilian law admits two different non-profit entities forms, the so-called associations and foundations. They differ from partnerships, limited liability companies and corporations in that they lack a profit motive. They are incorporated for the development of charitable, cultural or artistic objectives or, more generally, on behalf of the public welfare.

An association groups persons. In terms of Article 61 of the BCC, upon dissolution, the assets of an association, unless otherwise determined by its by-laws, should be vested in federal, state or municipal government institutions, the objectives of which are similar to those of the legal entity extinguished, or to the federal, state or municipal treasury themselves, in case no institution with similar purposes exists. In Brazil, trade unions are organized as associations as per Articles 511 and 518 of the Brazilian Consolidation of Labour Laws.

The BCC also regulates, in Articles 62 through 69, the so-called foundation, which is different from the association due to the fact that it groups chattels and/or real estate, not persons. It is created by a public deed, which should declare the estate settled and the purpose of the creation of the foundation. It is also possible to indicate in the deed the way the foundation is to be administered. Once created, it will be under the compulsory supervision of a public attorney. Moreover, its by-laws may only be altered by the affirmative vote of two-thirds of those charged with its administration. Such alteration may not, in any case, turn the foundation away from the objectives declared upon its formation. Upon winding up, the assets of a foundation shall be vested upon another foundation with similar objectives, unless the by-laws of the former provide differently. The foundation cannot strictly be classified as a non-profit association since it has no members to which profits might be distributed. In practical terms, in Brazil, it plays a role similar to the trust in common-law jurisdictions.

Both associations and foundations depend on registration with the Civil Registrar of Legal Entities in order to be validly created (Article 45 of the BCC). The last form of non-corporate association is the so-called cooperative. Its typical objective is the rendering of services to its members, acquiring raw materials at prices more favourable than those of individual purchases due to the economy of scale involved, sale of production, and so on. Cooperatives are most commonly formed by agricultural producers. The basic legal regime applicable to cooperatives is defined by Law No. 5764, dated 16 December 1971 and Articles 1093 through 1096 of the BCC. According to such rules, cooperatives may have a variable capital. They must be constituted by individuals in a minimum number sufficient for the administration of the company. The liability of the members may be limited or not, according to the provisions of the by-laws of the cooperative. The quotas of the company may not be transferred to third parties. Three administrative organs are charged with conducting a cooperative's business: the general meeting of its members, with deliberative functions; the Board of Directors; and the Board of Officers.

§4. Sources and Hierarchy of the Law on Corporations, Limited Liability Companies, and Partnerships

I. International Sources

14. In Brazil, rules on corporations and partnerships arise mainly from internal law sources. External treaties or rules from international organizations play no important role in this scenario.

II. Basic Internal Sources

15. Under the terms of Article 22, sub-item I and Article 48 of the Brazilian Federal Constitution, the Brazilian Federation, through the National Congress, has the exclusive right to legislate civil and commercial law. This terminology is broad enough to include legislation regarding business associations. Pursuant to this rule, the law of business associations is contained in federal statutes. The most important of such statutes are the already mentioned BCC (rules relating to limited liability companies and partnerships) and BCA (rules relating to corporations and limited partnerships by shares).

III. The Role of Case Law

16. As is typical in civil law systems, court decisions are theoretically deemed to interpret the law, not to expand it. However, such expansion may take place in order to fill statutory gaps under the terms of Article 4 of Law of Introduction to the Rules of Brazilian Law (*Lei de Introdução às Normas do Direito Brasileiro*, Decree Law No. 4657, dated 4 September 1942). In this case, the decision should be guided by analogy, customs, and the general principles of law. These rules apply without exception to the law of business associations.

IV. Law Versus Contractual Clauses

17. It is necessary to explain the relation between legal provisions and the documents filed in the incorporation of a corporation or the formation of limited liability companies and partnerships. It must at this point be stressed that the law of business associations, as a chapter of private law, is governed by the so-called waivable rights principle. This means that, as a general rule, legal provisions may be altered by by-laws and articles of association.

Some provisions are, however, included in the legislation in view of the public interest, and thus, their application cannot be avoided by private covenants. These are especially common in relation to corporations, since the BCA has adopted an institutionalist approach to them; that is, it views them as entities of society that should regard public welfare and interest, as well as self-interest, in their dealings. As a general rule, legal provisions creating rules protecting creditors, minority shareholders, partners, or employees, as well as those imposing fiduciary duties or liabilities on officers and controlling shareholders or partners, cannot be altered by the internal statutory or contractual provisions.

§5. International Private Law

I. Rules of Thumb

18. The basic rule of conflict applied to legal entities in Brazil, including corporations, limited liability companies, and partnerships, is that these entities are regulated by the law of the place of their incorporation or formation (Article 11 of the Law of Introduction to the Rules of Brazilian Law). This rule cannot, however, be accepted without one qualification. Under the terms of Article 60 of Decree Law No. 2627, dated 26 September 1940, a legal entity cannot be considered Brazilian unless it is administered from Brazil. This provision has, as a matter of practice, been granted a restrictive and liberal construction implying only the obligation to hold shareholders' and directors' meetings in Brazil. In this sense, Brazilian courts tend not to deem a legal entity as foreign when it is registered in Brazil and has its executive administration here (officers and managers) but is effectively controlled from abroad. At any rate, it must be borne in mind that the exclusion of applicability of Brazilian law to foreign corporations, limited liability companies, and partnerships refers exclusively to those provisions regarding the organization and functioning of business associations as such. Obviously, their dealings in Brazil involving general civil or commercial law aspects will not necessarily be subject to foreign law but rather be governed by the legal system indicated in the applicable private international law rules of conflicts of laws. Moreover, even in the realm of the law relating to business entities, foreign law shall not apply whenever its provisions deny Brazilian sovereignty or are deleterious to the public order (Article 17 of the Law of Introduction to the Rules of Brazilian Law). In relation to companies and partnerships, case law explaining how such limitations tend to be understood is scant. They would typically be applied to prevent the influence of the law of an enemy country in times of war.

II. Operation of Foreign Business Entities in Brazil Through Branches

19. Foreign corporations, limited liability companies, and partnerships are not prohibited as a general rule from operating through a branch in Brazil. For such purpose, they should have the documents filed with their incorporation papers abroad previously approved by the federal government under the terms of Article 11, first paragraph of the Law of Introduction to the Rules of Brazilian Law.

In practical terms, such approval is to be issued by the Ministry of State Development, Industry, Trade and Services (the jurisdiction of such ministry was delegated by the President of Brazil through Decree No. 11497, dated 20 April 2023) which may further delegate this authority to the Director of the Department of Commerce Registration and Integration (DREI) – a subordinate entity to the Special Secretariat of Micro and Small Companies and Entrepreneurship of the Ministry of Development, Industry, Trade and Services. For the purpose of issuance of this authorization, applicants shall present to DREI, along with the request for the authorization, a substantial number of documents and statements, including corporate minutes and financial statements, as well as the appointment of a representative in Brazil and the destination of the necessary capital for the development of the business of the local branch (DREI Normative Ruling No. 77, dated 18 March 2020).

There are more disadvantages than advantages in the creation of local Brazilian branches, which explains why this structure is rarely chosen as a form of organization for foreign businesses in the country. The disadvantages are: (i) the request for the authorization may be refused on a discretionary basis; (ii) there is no foreseeable term for the issuance of the authorization; (iii) the excessive number of documents and statements required by the Ministry of Development, Industry, Trade and Services; (iv) the high costs involved in the publication of documents and statements; and (v) the difficulties in comparison with the formation of limited liability companies and corporations. However, the very material advantage of incorporating a local branch in Brazil consists in the possibility of presentation of the economic, technical, and financial qualifications of foreign companies, on behalf of their local branches, in bid proceedings promoted by governmental entities.

As for taxation, any Brazilian branches, agencies, representations, or sales offices of legal entities domiciled out of Brazil are basically subject to the same corporate taxation applicable to Brazilian legal entities. Local agents or representatives acting in Brazil to the benefit of foreign legal entities may also, in certain cases, be regarded as permanent establishments of the foreign legal entity, thus subjecting the local income of the foreign legal entity to Brazilian corporate taxation (for which the agent is liable). In some cases, the taxable income of the foreign legal entity can be arbitrated for Brazilian taxation purposes.

III. Brazilian Business Association with Foreign Capital and the Applicable Limits

20. Foreign legal entities or individuals may also participate as shareholders, members, or partners in Brazilian corporations, limited liability companies, and partnerships. This participation is free in principle. It may, however, be restricted or limited in cases of companies operating in sectors considered sensitive to national security or interests. These sectors or activities include, among others, the following: television channels, radio stations and the press (Article 222 of the Federal Constitution), mining (Article 176, first paragraph of the Federal Constitution), etc. As to the participation of foreigners in Brazilian financial institutions (banks), Article 192 of the Federal Constitution provides that special statutes, not yet prepared, shall regulate the matter.[12] Such regulation shall take into account both Brazilian economic interests and obligations under international treaties.

§6. Labour Law Connection

I. Profit Sharing Bonus

21. Law No. 10101, dated 19 December 2000, was enacted to regulate the participation of workers in the profits of private and state-owned enterprises. As per Article 3 of the referred law, payments to workers as profit participations are tax deductible and cannot be made more than twice in the same civil year and in intervals shorter than three months.

The amount of the profit sharing bonus established according to the provisions of Law No. 10101/00 is not considered salary and, as a consequence, does not have to be included in the calculation of the labour benefits (Christmas bonus, vacation bonus, deposits in the account of the Severance Guarantee Fund (*Fundo de Garantia do Tempo de Serviço–* FGTS), and so on) and the social security contributions.

Law No. 10101/00 sets forth that the profit sharing plan shall have clear and objective rules regarding the form of payment, frequency of the distribution, term of effectiveness, term for the review of the plan and goals to be achieved by the participating workers. In addition, the Law sets forth that the profit sharing plan shall be created by a collective bargaining agreement or by a commission chosen by the parties, a member of such commission being mandatorily a representative of the relevant employees' Union.

Profit sharing bonus is subject to Withholding Income Tax (WHT), exclusively at source, at specific progressive rates ranging from 0% to 27.5% (payments up to BRL 7,407.11 are currently exempt).

---

12. Article 52 of the Temporary Constitutional Provisions Act sets forth that, until the conditions of Art. 192 are created, the following is prohibited: (i) the installation in Brazil of new branches of financial institutions domiciled abroad; and (ii) the increase in the percentage of interest in financial institutions domiciled in Brazil by individuals or entities domiciled abroad. These prohibitions, however, are not applicable when authorized as a result of international treaties, reciprocity or interests of the Brazilian government. The latter exception has been recently extended to encompass all requests of participation in local financial institutions or the installation of local branches, as per Law No. 10029/22 and Circular No. 3977/20, from the Central Bank of Brazil.

II. Stock Option Plans

22. Brazil still does not have specific legislation regarding stock options granted by companies to workers,[13] except for Law No. 12,973/14, which regulated the tax deductibility of these payments from the calculation basis of corporate income taxes due by the granting company. There are also Technical Pronouncements enacted by the Brazilian Accounting Pronouncements Committee (CPC), based on IFRS guidelines, providing specific accounting treatment for share-based payments made by Brazilian entities.

Brazilian Labour Courts usually held that stock options are not part of the salary (for purposes of calculating labour benefits) provided that: (i) the options are not granted to the employees as a form of compensation for services rendered, since the granting is not linked to the performance of the employees; (ii) the employees do not receive shares for free, but rather have to actually purchase them (even if the purchase price is fixed at the date of the granting of the options with a discount); and (iii) the value of the shares is subject to market fluctuation, since as a result of these characteristics at the end of the vesting period the employees may have a profit or a loss with the sale of shares acquired by them.

Brazilian tax authorities historically have a restrictive approach regarding tax implications of share-based compensation paid to employees. Broadly speaking, unless a given share-based payment (settled in stock or cash) is completely unrelated to the employee's services, it should be considered service compensation for all tax and social security purposes in Brazil.

However, recent judgments by the Superior Court of Administrative Tax Appeals (CSRF) show a more flexible approach, considering stock options to have a mercantile/commercial nature instead of considering them as service compensation, provided certain characteristics are present. Court precedents that take this position usually demand certain conditions similar to those applied by Labour Courts and listed above to be met so that payments made under share-based compensation plans can be treated as stock transactions rather than service compensation.

III. Disregard of Legal Entity by the Labour Courts

23. Although Labour courts have systematically shown a tendency to disregard the legal identity of a company and use the property of its partners for redress in the event the company's assets are not sufficient to meet its debts, new laws have been subtly reducing labour liability risks.

The so-called Labour Reform, that became effective at the end of 2017, enhanced legal certainty for former shareholders. The new law has limited the extent of the liability of a former shareholder for labour obligations to a period of two years as from the date the shareholder ceases to hold shares. In addition, it established that

13. Such a regulation is being discussed in the Brazilian Congress, as of the end of 2023 (Senate's Bill No. 2724/2022).

former shareholders are liable in a secondary manner ('responsabilidade subsidiária'), i.e., they can only be held liable should the company and current shareholders lack assets to guarantee and/or pay the labour debts. In addition to that, the Law on Economic Freedom aims at the simplification of business activities and sets out that shareholders shall only be held liable for corporate debts in general when they benefit directly or indirectly from the abuse of the corporate personality. This provision protects minority shareholders from benefitting from looting of corporate assets. Even considering that this provision may be refused application as a matter of fact by Labour Courts, there is a likelihood of a positive influence on the business climate.

24. Despite being less common, decisions for which the managers of the company were considered liable for labour debts have also been identified.

IV. Liability of Controlling Shareholders Towards Employees

25. Please also *see* §3 above.

V. Voluntary Attribution of Interests to Employees

26. Brazilian company statutes also provide for non-compulsory means for the participation of workers, if desired by the employer. The first paragraph of Article 140 of the BCA states that the by-laws of any corporation can establish the participation of a representative of the workers on the Board of Directors.

Another vehicle of worker participation in privately held corporations (no other corporate form can issue such bond) is the so-called profit participation bond (*parte beneficiária*), which is a security that can be issued by a privately held corporation in favour of foundations or charities to the benefit of its employees (Article 47 of the BCA). Such securities confer on their holders the right to share profits but bear no voting rights. This can, however, be remedied by the issuance of these profit participation bonds convertible into shares (Article 48, second paragraph, of the BCA). Profit participation bonds do not represent share capital prior to their conversion into shares, but such conversion is possible in case a suitable reserve is formed with the companies' own funds and then incorporated in the share capital.

At any rate, the frequency of the participation of workers and co-determination in Brazil is very low. Although provisions for the participation of workers in the profits have been introduced in our legal system, mandatory co-determination rules are still non-existent. Rules towards at least some limited form of co-determination should, in our opinion, be introduced in the legislation. Pursuant to such rules, workers' influence would be escalated and grow in proportion to the administrative ability shown in individual cases. For such purposes, a means of measuring such administrative ability in individual cases would have to be provided for and developed in legislation, a not-so-simple problem that goes beyond the limited scope of this work.

Part I. Corporations

Chapter 1. 'Sociedades Anônimas' (Corporations)

§1. INCORPORATION

I. Introduction

27. Corporations represent one of the most common corporate structures utilized for business purposes in Brazil. It is also the structure required for a company that intends to have its shares traded on the stock exchanges. However, for that purpose, a number of additional requirements, including governmental authorization, must be met. This will be considered later with respect to publicly held companies (paragraph 31 below).

Due to the relative simplicity involved in the transfer of its shares, which facilitates its sale to the public, the corporation is undoubtedly the most regulated corporate structure found in Brazilian law, beginning with its incorporation procedures and requirements, as seen below.

II. Preliminary Requirements

28. The requirements and procedures for the formation of a corporation are regulated in Chapters VII and VIII, Articles 80–99 of the BCA. Three preliminary conditions are imposed.

The first of such conditions is the subscription of all shares of the capital stock set forth in the by-laws; such subscription is to be effected by at least two persons (Article 80, item I). Although the law refers only to '*persons*', the meaning implies both individuals and legal entities. The minimum initial number of two subscribers shall be kept regardless of its type or class.

Accordingly, as per Article 206, item I sub-item 'd' of the BCA, one of the reasons for a corporation's mandatory winding up is verification, during an ordinary general shareholders' meeting, that the corporation has only one shareholder, except in the case of wholly owned subsidiaries – as described below. Winding up will then occur in the event that the minimum number of two shareholders is not re-established until the next ordinary shareholders' meeting.

The second preliminary requirement established by Article 80 for the formation of a corporation is the imposition of a minimum percentage of the subscription price that must be paid immediately in currency. Generally, such a minimum is 10%

(Article 80, item II). Notwithstanding, it may be raised for specific types of corporations, as defined in federal law (Article 80, sole paragraph, of the BCA).

The shareholders of financial institutions, for instance, must pay 50% of the amount of the subscription immediately. This will apply either in the case of an initial subscription, when the payment must be made in currency, or in the subscription of a later increase of the institution's capital stock (Article 27 of Law No. 4595, dated 31 December 1964, which regulates the Brazilian financial market).

As will be discussed later on, the capital may be divided into shares with or without a par value (Article 11 of the BCA). If the shares are issued bearing a par value, the subscription price may be higher than such a value. Even if the shares do not bear a par value, the subscription price may surpass the proportional value each share represents in the total corporate capital.

Indeed, as will be discussed in item 41, the BCA establishes that a premium may be charged to the subscribers, the corresponding value to be allotted not to the corporation's capital but to capital reserves, as per Articles 13, second paragraph, and 182, first paragraph, of the BCA. However, it shall be stressed that the subscription price may never be lower than the par value (Article 13 of the BCA).

Finally, the last of the three preliminary requirements established by the BCA for setting up a corporation is that all funds received in currency for the payment of the corporation's capital upon its formation must be deposited with the *Banco do Brasil S.A.* (a federally owned commercial bank) or with any other bank authorized by the Securities Commission (CVM) for that specific purpose (Article 80, item III, of the BCA).

The CVM is a regulatory agency under the authority of the Ministry of Finance. It is responsible for the regulation and supervision of the securities market, as well as for the management of the registries necessary for participation in this market, as defined by Law No. 6385, dated 7 December 1976.

Above the CVM in the hierarchy of governmental economic agencies is the National Monetary Council (CMN), created by Law No. 4595, dated 31 December 1964, for the purpose of defining the national policy as to currency and credit (Article 2) in accordance with the directives established by the President of the Republic (Article 4).

In accordance with Article 81 of the BCA, the deposits referred to above must be made by a representative of the subscribers of the corporation being formed, called an incorporator, within five days from the receipt of the corresponding amounts from the initial subscribers.[14] Such a deposit is to be made in the name of the respective subscriber, in favour of the corporation in the process of formation, through a bank deposit, to be withdrawn only by the company, except in the case described in the last paragraph of this section.

14. The incorporator is the person who makes all efforts to gather the initial subscribers for the specific purpose of setting up the corporation. He arranges for the fulfilment of all legal requirements, the preparation of the necessary documents, the preliminary draft of the by-laws, and in the case of a corporation formed by means of public subscription, he will also arrange for the necessary registration with the CVM, as will be explained in para. 28. The incorporators may be subscribers or not. The incorporators are to deliver to the first managers of the corporation all documents pertinent to its incorporation (Art. 93 of the BCA). The incorporators, as well as, in the case of public subscriptions, the financial institution whose participation is mandatory (*see* para. 28), are liable, within their

The corporation will only be allowed to withdraw the aforesaid bank deposit after its incorporation has been completed and the status of a legal entity has been acquired. In accordance with Article 45 of the BCC, a company acquires personality for legal purposes, and therefore, the status of a legal entity, by filing its incorporation acts with the pertinent public registry.

As per the sole paragraph of Article 982 of the BCC, whatever its purposes are, the corporation will always bear an entrepreneurial nature. Therefore, its incorporation acts are to be filed with the Commercial Registry of the Brazilian State, where the company has its headquarters.

In the event that the corporation is not duly formed within six months from the date the deposit was made, through the filing of the incorporation acts and documents with the Commercial Registry and their subsequent publication, the amounts deposited must be returned directly to the subscribers (Article 81, sole paragraph, of the BCA).

III. Incorporation by Means of Public Subscription

29. Corporations may be formed by means of public subscription of their capital. In this case, authorization by the CVM is required pursuant to Article 82 of the BCA. In addition, the participation of a financial institution as an intermediary is necessary.

According to Article 82, first paragraph, of the BCA, the request to the CVM for said authorization, besides complying with the standards established by the CVM itself, shall be accompanied by: (i) a report on the economic viability of the project; (ii) a draft of the by-laws; and (iii) a prospectus, organized and executed by the incorporators and by the financial institution serving as an intermediary (*see* paragraph 46 below).

The registration for distribution of shares by means of public issuance is regulated by the CVM in its Resolution No. 160 dated 13 July 2022 (as amended by CVM Resolution No. 173 dated 29 November 2022, CVM Resolution No. 180 dated 22 March 2023 and CVM Resolution No. 183 dated 11 May 2023), which basically imposes a number of documents to be presented and procedures to be followed in order to guarantee effective and precise disclosure of the corporation's standing, so that future subscribers may make the best decision in accordance with their expectations. Notwithstanding, the CVM may condition the issuance of a registration on amendments to the by-laws and/or to the prospectus or even deny such a registration considering the enterprise's lack of chance of success or because of the incorporator's bad reputation (Article 82, second paragraph, of the BCA).

The draft of the by-laws shall meet all legal requirements applicable to contracts of companies in general and specifically to corporations. It shall also comprise the articles that are to govern the corporation's future activities (Article 83 of the BCA), its contents indicated in paragraph 31 below.

---

respective assignments, for any loss eventually originated from the disregard of any legal provisions. All the incorporators of a corporation are also jointly liable for any loss caused, intentionally or not, through their acts or operations prior to the incorporation (Art. 92 of the BCA).

Once subscription is determined and it is verified that the corporate capital has been fully subscribed, the incorporators must call for a general shareholders' meeting for the purpose of appraising the goods received as payment of capital, if necessary (*see* paragraph 36 below) and definitively resolving to incorporate the enterprise (Article 86 of the BCA).

The calling for the general shareholders' meeting shall indicate the time, date, and address where the shareholders' meeting is to take place and shall be published in the same newspapers in which the offerings of subscription were effected (Article 86, sole paragraph, of the BCA).

The initial general shareholders' meeting will begin at the first call when subscribers representing at least half of the corporation's capital are present. At the second call, the meeting will begin with any number of subscribers (Article 87 of the BCA).

One of the incorporators is to preside over the initial shareholders' meeting, while any subscriber may serve as secretary. The subscribers will then debate and decide upon the adoption of the draft of the by-laws. For this initial meeting, every share bears voting rights, regardless of its kind. It should be pointed out that the draft of the by-laws may only be amended at this meeting by a resolution approved unanimously.

Once all legal requirements are accomplished, the chairman of the general shareholders' meeting is to declare the corporation duly incorporated, unless subscribers representing more than 50% of the corporation's capital oppose such declaration. The administrators of the corporation and the members of its Board of Auditors will then be appointed during the meeting.

Minutes of the meeting are drafted by the president and the secretary of the meeting and read to all the participants. After approval, the minutes are prepared for filing with the Commercial Registry and are transcribed in the corporate book of the company and executed by all the shareholders present or, at least, by shareholders who represent the minimum valid quorum for the resolutions adopted.

IV. Incorporation by Means of Private Subscription

30. Private subscriptions in Brazil are much less regulated than public subscriptions since they do not involve funding with public savings. Article 88 of the BCA states that incorporation by private subscription may be performed through a resolution of the subscribers in a general shareholders' meeting or by means of a public deed. In the latter case, all of the initial subscribers are deemed incorporators.

The subscriber may appoint an attorney-in-fact with specific powers to represent him/her in the subscriber's initial meeting or in the public deed leading to the formation of a corporation (Article 90 of the BCA).

If the incorporation by deed method is adopted, the second paragraph of Article 88 of the BCA establishes a list of data that is to be mentioned in such a deed, namely: (i) subscribers' particulars; (ii) by-laws; (iii) list of subscribed shares and amounts paid in; (iv) copy of the receipt of a bank deposit attesting payment of the subscription price; (v) in case of subscriptions that involve the paying up of the capital in goods, a copy of the respective appraisal record (*see* paragraph 36 hereof);

and (vi) the nomination of the first members of the management, and, if the case should be, the members of the fiscal committee.

V. Contents of the By-Laws of a Corporation

31. As seen above, both privately held corporations and publicly held corporations require by-laws in order to be incorporated. The following matters, among others, are to be addressed in the by-laws:

- corporate purpose, precisely and completely indicated (Article 2, second paragraph, of the BCA);
- corporate capital, to be expressed in national currency (Article 5 of the BCA);
- number of shares into which the capital is divided and whether or not the shares have a nominal/par value (Article 11 of the BCA – *see* paragraph 37 below);
- the rights applicable to each class of shares (Articles 16, 16-A and 17 of the BCA);
- right of one or more classes of preferred shares to appoint a certain number of members of the administrative bodies (if applicable) (Article 18 of the BCA);
- the fact that amendments to the by-laws in relation to certain subjects are conditioned to approval of one or more classes of preferred shareholders (if applicable) (sole paragraph of Article 18 of the BCA);
- benefits and restrictions of the preferred shares in comparison to ordinary shares (Article 19 of the BCA – *see* paragraph 38);
- form of the shares and indication of whether one form may be converted into the other (Article 22 of the BCA – *see* paragraph 41);
- classes of shares that will be kept deposited in a depository institution (Article 34 of the BCA – *see* paragraph 42), and authorization to the depositor to charge the shareholders for transfer services within the limits imposed by the CVM (if applicable) (Article 35, third paragraph, of the BCA);
- for privately held corporations only, and under certain legal conditions, limitations on the transferability of registered shares (if applicable) (Article 36 of the BCA);
- procedure for paying retiring shareholders in the cases admitted by the law (if applicable) (Article 45, first paragraph, of the BCA);
- duration and benefits of the profit participation bonds and creation of reserves to redeem the same (if applicable) (Articles 48 and 49, item V, of the BCA);
- authorization for the Board of Directors to issue subscription bonds (*see* paragraph 64) without the need for approval by the general shareholders' meeting (if applicable) (Articles 76 and 142, item VII, of the BCA);
- limitation on the maximum number of votes of each shareholder (if applicable) (Article 110, first paragraph, of the BCA);
- creation of super voting ordinary shares (if applicable) (Article 110-A of the BCA);
- limitation on voting (and/or other) rights of preferred shares (if applicable) (Article 111 of the BCA – *see* paragraph 38);

- in privately held companies only, a higher quorum for resolutions of general shareholders' meetings with respect to specific matters (if applicable) (Articles 129, first paragraph, and 136 of the BCA);
- with respect to the Board of Directors: number of members (minimum of three) admitted, and how the chairman is to be appointed and substituted; how the members are to be substituted; term of office, which shall not be longer than three years, re-election being admitted; organizational rules as to shareholders' meetings (Article 140 of the BCA – *see* paragraph 75);
- with respect to the officers, the number of officers (minimum of two), how they are to be substituted, term of office, which shall not be longer than three years, re-election being admitted, and the powers and duties of each officer (Article 143 of the BCA – *see* paragraph 76);
- whether the members of the administrative bodies (Board of Directors, if applicable, and officers) shall pledge shares of the company or present other kinds of surety to guarantee the performance of their duties (if applicable) (Article 148 of the BCA);
- right of such members of the administrative bodies to participate in the profits, provided that a minimum annual dividend of not less than 25% of the net profits is established in the by-laws (if applicable) (Article 152, first paragraph, of the BCA);
- regulations as to the functioning of the Board of Auditors (Article 161 of the BCA);
- authorized capital up to which subscriptions may be made without need for amendments to the by-laws (if applicable) (Article 168 of the BCA – *see* paragraph 33);
- with respect to distribution of profits, creation and specification as to reserves, in addition to the reserves set forth by the BCA (Article 194 of the BCA);
- minimum mandatory annual dividend (if not indicated in the by-laws, it will be 50% of the net profits after the established deductions) (Article 202 of the BCA – *see* paragraph 73);
- cases in which the corporation will be wound up, in addition to the events already mentioned by the BCA (if applicable) (Article 206, item I, sub-item 'b', of the BCA); and
- liquidation procedures (if applicable) (Article 208 of the BCA – *see* paragraphs 91–95).

VI. Acts Complementary to the Incorporation

32. Chapter VIII of the BCA establishes a number of formalities to complement the corporation's incorporation. Article 94 states that no corporation may carry out business before its incorporation acts are duly filed (with the Commercial Registry) and published (*see* paragraph 28). The acts to be filed with the Commercial Registry are fully specified in Articles 95 and 96 and basically correspond to documents evidencing that all legal requirements mentioned above for the incorporation of the corporation were met.

Indeed, it is the Commercial Registry's function, before bringing to public knowledge the existence of the corporation, to ascertain whether all legal requirements were fully met in order to consider the corporation as validly incorporated. If they are not met, the Registry may disallow the filing of the incorporation acts. In this case, a general meeting shall be immediately called by the first administrators appointed in order to resolve the missing requirements and, eventually, determine whether or not indemnification for losses should be claimed by the incorporators (Article 97 of the BCA).

Once the incorporation documents have been duly filed, the administrators must arrange with the government's official gazette and with a local newspaper for the publication of their contents within thirty days, together with the Registry's certificate of filing. Thereafter, copies of both publications are to be filed with the same Registry of Commerce (Article 98 of the BCA).

Finally, Article 99 of the BCA states that the first administrators are jointly liable for any losses eventually caused by any delay in fulfilling the full complement of formalities of incorporating the corporation. The corporation is not responsible for acts undertaken by the first administrators prior to the fulfilment of the incorporation formalities unless the general shareholders' meeting resolves on the contrary. Any contractual obligations undertaken by the first administrators will remain their sole liability in the absence of any of the formalities described above. No joint and several liability will bind the incorporators to such obligations. The effect of such obligations will be restricted to those administrators who have been parties to the contract from which they were issued. This is a result of Article 265 of the BCC, in which terms joint and several liability can only be created by legal provisions or by the express consent of the parties involved, requirements absent in pre-incorporation contracts.

§2. Capital and Shares

I. Introduction

33. As seen above, the liability of the shareholder of a corporation is limited to the price paid or promised to be paid for the shares to which the same shareholder subscribed (Article 1 of the BCA). It is therefore relevant for the present study to make a brief comment as to how the corporate capital is formed as well as on the main characteristics of the shares in which such capital is divided.

II. Capital: Amount

34. In a corporation, the capital stock is established by the by-laws. The by-laws also regulate the procedures according to which, within the limits permitted by the law itself, the capital may be modified (Articles 5 and 6 of the BCA).

The by-laws may alternatively fix the authorized capital, which is the amount up to which the capital may be increased without the need for an amendment to the by-laws. When such authorization is provided, the by-laws must also indicate whether the resolution determining the increase in the capital is to be taken by the general shareholders' meeting or by the Board of Directors (Article 168 of the BCA).

The capital may only be increased after at least three-quarters of its subscription price has been paid (Article 170 of the BCA). The price for which new shares representing the increase in the capital are issued must reflect severally or alternatively one of the following criteria: (i) the price of the corporation's shares in the market, if that is the case; (ii) the actual value of the corporation's net worth; or (iii) the corporation's profitability perspectives. These criteria aim to prevent the existing shareholders from suffering an unreasonable or unjustified proportional decrease in the value of their shares (Article 170, first paragraph, of the BCA).

III. Right of First Refusal in the Subscription of New Shares

35. Shareholders have the right of first refusal in the subscription of new shares resulting from an increase in the capital, such right existing in relation to a number of shares proportional to their participation in the capital stock (Article 171 of the BCA).

Such right of first refusal will normally be exercised through the subscription of shares of the same class and type as those held by the shareholder, although such subscription may fall upon other classes in the event that the issuance of new shares is not made proportionally in all classes (Article 171, first paragraph, of the BCA).

The by-laws or the general shareholders' meeting shall establish the term, not less than thirty days, within which such right of first refusal in the subscription of new shares may be exercised (Article 171, fourth paragraph, of the BCA).

It is worth mentioning that the shareholder who intends not to exercise a right of first refusal may transfer such right to third parties (Article 171, sixth paragraph, of the BCA).

An exception to the rule of the right of first refusal is found in Article 172 of the BCA, according to which the by-laws of a publicly held company with authorized capital may allow the issuance of shares without such right, provided that the sale of the issued shares is made in the stock exchanges or such shares will be given in exchange for existing shares in public takeover bids.

IV. Payment in Goods

36. The capital of a corporation may be paid either in currency or in goods (Article 7 of the BCA). In the latter case, a detailed appraisal prepared by three recognized experts or a company expert in evaluating the goods given in payment for the capital is required in relation to the real estate or chattels incorporated in the corporation. Such experts or expert companies are to be appointed by the general shareholders' meeting and/or subscribers (future shareholders) according to a number of formal procedures indicated in Article 8 of the BCA.

The general shareholders' meeting must approve the value assigned to the goods by the appraisal. Thereafter, the subscriber who is offering the goods must accept the value approved by the general shareholders' meeting.

Notwithstanding those strict procedures that intend to avoid any possible fraud, both the subscriber and the appraisal experts are responsible for any losses eventually caused to the corporation, to other shareholders and/or subscribers, and to third parties in virtue of any distortion of the value assigned to the subscriber's goods.

Furthermore, it is worth mentioning that whenever the capital is paid by assignment of credits, the subscriber or shareholder will be held responsible for the debtor's solvency (Article 10, sole paragraph, of the BCA).

In addition, it must be pointed out that, in accordance with Brazilian law, property consisting of movable assets is normally transferred by their physical delivery to the transferee (Article 1267 of the BCC). However, there are some kinds of assets that may be subject to registration with specific Public Registries or public entities (e.g., vehicles whose certificates of title are to be amended by the local Traffic Department).

With respect to immovable assets, such as land, the transfer must be made by means of a public notary deed duly registered with the competent Real Estate Registry. However, when the transfer of real estate refers to payment of the capital of the corporation, Article 89 of the BCA establishes that a public deed will not be required.

V. Shares: Par Value

37. The number of shares into which the capital stock of a corporation is divided must be established in its by-laws. The by-laws shall also indicate whether or not the shares are issued at a par value (Article 11 of the BCA), which is equivalent to the division of the value of the company's capital for the total number of shares. If such is the case, the stated par value must be equal for all shares.

Even the by-laws of a corporation that does not issue shares bearing a par value may create a certain class of preferred shares with par value. The par value of shares issued by publicly held companies may not be lower than the minimum fixed by the CVM.

A corporation may not issue shares for a price lower than the par value, if it exists, but only equal to or higher than this value (Article 13 of the BCA). The reason for this rule is clear. A situation in which a corporation states a capital higher than its real available assets should always be avoided.

However, any payment exceeding the par value will be allotted not to capital but to capital surpluses (Articles 13, second paragraph, and 182, first paragraph, of the BCA). Such a rule is justified by the fact that the par value of a share precisely represents that stated capital divided by the number of shares. Therefore, any amount surpassing the par value cannot be accounted for as capital, even though it is in fact a surplus belonging to all the shareholders, proportional to their respective stakes.

Even in the case of shares not bearing a par value, a portion of the subscription price may be directed to capital surplus instead of being fully allocated to capital

(Article 14 of the BCA). The formation of a capital surplus usually occurs when the company's assets are not fully reflected in its stated capital but are nonetheless reflected in the price of the shares.

If the shares are to be issued without par value, their subscription price will be fixed either by the incorporators (initial subscriptions) or by the general shareholders' meeting (increases of capital).

VI. Types of Shares

38. Depending on the rights conferred upon their holders, the shares of a corporation are divided into three different types: preferred, ordinary, and fruitive (Article 15).

A. Preferred Shares

39. The minimum rights of a preferred shareholder will depend on whether the share is admitted to public negotiation or not. Publicly held corporations that do not negotiate preferred shares on the securities market or privately held companies can choose to attribute one of the following advantages to the preferred shares: (i) priority in the distribution of fixed or minimum dividends; (ii) priority in refunding capital, with or without premium; or (iii) accumulation of the rights provided in items (i) and (ii) (Article 17, items I, II, and III of the BCA).

However, preferred shares without the right to vote or that bear restrictions on the exercise of this right may only be negotiated in the securities market if at least one of the following characteristics are attributed to them: (i) the right to participate in the dividends to be distributed, which may not be less than 25% of the net profit for the fiscal year, with priority to receiving an amount equivalent to at least 3% of the equity value of the shares; (ii) the right to receive dividends at least 10% higher than those distributed for common shares; or (iii) the right to be included in the public offer for the sale of controlling interest, as well as the right to a dividend at least equivalent to that distributed for common shares (Article 17, first paragraph, of the BCA).

The preferred shares may be issued in various classes (Article 15, first paragraph, of the BCA), and the by-laws may grant to one or more of those classes the right to appoint one or more members of the management bodies – Board of Directors and/ or officers (Article 18 of the BCA). All the shares of the same class confer equal rights to all their holders (Article 109, first paragraph, of the BCA).

The by-laws, however, may deny the preferred shareholders one or more rights conferred upon ordinary shares (Article 111 of the BCA). Among those, the by-laws may hinder or partially restrict voting rights. However, such hindrances or restrictions will be suspended in the event that the corporation does not pay the fixed or minimum dividends for a certain period. Such a period is to be indicated in the by-laws and shall not be longer than three years. It should be mentioned that the by-laws may also determine that the period in question will not be counted until the company is ready to carry on business, that is, during the so-called pre-operational period.

The number of preferred shares subject to any restriction as to voting rights may not exceed 50% of the aggregate number of shares issued by the corporation (Article 15, second paragraph, of the BCA).

B. Ordinary Shares

40. Ordinary shares are those to which the by-laws may neither extend the preferences nor impose the restrictions mentioned above for the preferred shares.

The privately held corporation may have its ordinary shares divided into classes, depending on: (i) the possibility of their conversion into preferred shares; (ii) the existence of a requirement of their holders having Brazilian nationality; or (iii) the qualified voting right to appoint members for certain positions of the management bodies (Article 16, items I, II, and III, of the BCA).

Generally, publicly held corporations are not allowed to create multiple classes of common stock, except for the adoption of super voting shares as introduced by Law No. 14195 dated 26 August 2021 (Article 16-A of the BCA).

Corporations in Brazil may have super voting ordinary shares, allowing the concentration of political power. Super voting ordinary shares have stronger are those bearing voting rights without correspondence to the capital invested.

Both privately held and publicly held corporations can implement super voting shares, but in the case of publicly held corporations, this must occur prior to the trading of any shares or securities convertible into shares on organized securities markets (Article 110-A, items I, II, and III of the BCA).

Super voting shares cannot grant more than ten votes per share (Article 110-A of the BCA).

Except for super voting shares, all ordinary shares of the same class must be granted equal rights (first paragraph of Article 109 of the BCA). The by-laws may also declare preferred shares to be convertible into ordinary shares and vice versa (Article 19 of the BCA).

In the context of different classes of shares, be they preferred or ordinary, it is worth mentioning the existence of golden shares in Brazil. The privatisation of state-owned companies during the 1990s was characterized by the creation of a special class of shares that became known as golden shares, giving the Brazilian government special political rights. Golden shares granted the Brazilian government veto rights over certain specific corporate matters, such as the veto over certain decisions and the right to appoint members of the management.

C. Fruitive Shares

41. Fruitive shares are those that do not represent a portion of the corporation's capital, merely conferring upon their holders the right to distribution of profits. That occurs by means of complete amortization of the shares, with the total amount of capital originally represented by the shares being fully returned to the shareholders. The operation according to which such amortizations occur is explained in paragraph 48 below.

VII. Form of Shares

42. With respect to their form, the BCA originally established that the shares of a corporation could either be vested by a nominal, endorsable, or bearer form (Article 20 of the BCA). However, Law No. 8021, dated 12 April 1990, abolished bearer shares, as well as all other securities issued to bearers, intending to avoid tax evasion and invigorate Brazilian federal tax revenues. Accordingly, Law No. 8021/90 amended Article 20 of the BCA to the effect that shares of corporations may only be issued in nominative form.

Therefore, nowadays, a corporation must control its securities either by keeping all the registries in relation to its securities in its corporate books or by delegating such a task to a registered deposit institution authorized by the CVM.

VIII. Share Certificates

43. Article 24 of the BCA indicates a number of terms that must be inscribed in the share certificate of a corporation. This data basically refers to particulars of the corporation, the amount of its capital, the number of shares into which said capital is divided, basic information as to the issuance of the share represented, and, of course, the shareholder's name.

The issuance of certificates is not mandatory. The registry of shares, or some classes of them, may only be kept in a registered deposit account on behalf of the shareholders with a depository institution authorized by the CVM or in the corporate books of the company without issuance of certificates.

The transfer of shares in the first case will be done by the depository institution in its records upon receipt of a written order from the respective registered shareholder. The depository institution is to provide the shareholders with statements of the deposit account from time to time (Articles 34 and 35 of the BCA).

IX. Negotiability of Shares

44. While the shares of privately held corporations may be negotiated immediately, as soon as 10% of the initial subscription is paid in (*see* paragraph 28 above), the shares of publicly held corporations are prevented from circulating until at least 30% of the subscription price is paid (Article 29 of the BCA).

The imposition of a minimum percentage of the subscription price to be paid before the sale of the shares of a publicly held corporation higher than the percentage applicable to privately held corporations is due to the fact that in that kind of corporation, shares circulate rapidly on the market, and therefore it may be more difficult to receive the total amount of the subscription price if a subscriber fails to fully pay the price. The rule thus aims at providing an additional guarantee that the corporation will have enough available funds to do business if failures to arrive at the subscription price occur. Also aimed at reducing such risk of failure, Article 108 of the BCA provides that, for a period of two years, the transferor shareholder and the new shareholder will be jointly liable for the outstanding payment of the subscription price.

The by-laws of privately held corporations may impose restrictions on the circulation of the shares of the corporation whether or not fully paid in, provided that such restrictions are clearly and precisely stated and provided that those restrictions neither imply an absolute ban on negotiation of the shares nor subordinate the shareholder to the sole discretion of the administrative bodies or of the majority of the shareholders (Article 36 of the BCA). If such restrictions are imposed by means of an amendment to the by-laws, they shall only apply to the shareholders (as well as to their successors and assignees) who give their express consent by an entry in the register of shares.

X. Public Issuance of Shares

45. Brazilian statutes provide strict protection to public savings against irregular offers of securities. Accordingly, regulations pertaining to financial and securities markets subject public issuances to the supervision of CVM.

Article 16 of Law No. 4728, dated 14 July 1965, imposes that such issuances be made through the distribution system indicated in Article 5 of the same law. According to said Article 5, the distribution system basically comprehends companies that operate in the financial or securities markets duly authorized for that purpose by the Central Bank of Brazil or by the CVM (i.e., commercial banks, investment banks, brokerage houses, and other similar institutions).

Law No. 6385, dated 7 December 1976, which created the CVM, specifically regulates the securities market. In accordance with Article 2 of this law and for its purposes, the meaning of the term 'securities' shall encompass the following:

- shares of stock, debentures, and subscription bonds (*see* paragraphs 38, 50 and 64 hereof);
- bonds, rights, subscription receipts, and stock split certificates related to the securities mentioned in item 26 above;
- certificates of deposit of securities;
- debenture notes;
- shares of funds for investment in securities or of associations for investment in any assets;
- commercial notes;
- future agreements, option agreements, and other derivatives whose subjacent assets are securities;
- other derivative agreements, regardless of the subjacent assets; and

– when publicly offered, any other collective titles or investment agreements that generate participation, partnership, or remuneration rights, including those resulting from the rendering of services whose revenues arise from the work of the entrepreneur or of third parties.

The first paragraph of Article 2 of Law No. 6385/76 expressly excludes from the meaning of securities: (i) federal, state, and municipal bonds of debt; and (ii) bills that represent liabilities of financial institutions, except for debentures.

Having defined the term 'security', it is worth mentioning that Article 19 of Law No. 6385/76 establishes that no public issuance of securities shall be distributed in the market – that is, publicly offered or sold through the distribution system – without previous registration before the CVM. This rule is specifically reinforced in Article 4, first paragraph, of the BCA, which establishes that only securities issued by corporations duly registered with the CVM may be distributed in the market and negotiated on the stock exchanges and on the over-the-counter market.

The registration of companies before the CVM shall be made pursuant to the CVM Resolution No. 80, dated 29 March 2022, which sets forth specific requirements of information disclosure applicable to the issuers of securities. According to such Resolution, all relevant information of the company must be made available through a comprehensive document named 'Reference Form'. The Reference Form is under permanent disclosure on the websites of the company and of the CVM, and it is updated within a seven-day term as of the occurrence of any event that changes its content.

Complementary Law No. 182/21, aiming to facilitate access to the capital market, established that CVM will regulate simplified conditions for small corporations to access the capital market, introducing Article 294-A to the BCA. A corporation is considered small if it earns annual gross revenue below R$ 500,000,000.00 (Article 294-B of the BCA). The obligations of fully regulated corporations that can be waived are: (i) the installation of a Board of Auditors at the request of shareholders; (ii) the intermediation of a financial institution in public offerings of securities; (iii) payment of mandatory dividends; and (iv) publication of corporate acts referred to in Article 289 of the BCA.

The effective granting of such benefits through CVM regulation has not been completed as of November 2023. So far, Resolution No. 166, dated 1 September 2022, was enacted to render concrete the advantages in the preceding paragraph, simplifying the regime of legal publications requirements. In addition, Resolution No. 168, dated 20 September 2022, created the possibility of cumulation of the positions of CEO and Chairman of the Board of Directors for publicly held small corporations.

For the registration of security offers to be approved, the party requiring it shall file, with the CVM, detailed information on the securities to be floated and present the contracts and documents basing the flotation, including the prospectus (paragraph 46 below), the stabilization agreement and the distribution agreement (Annex K of CVM Resolution No. 160/22).

There is, however, a simplified procedure for public flotations (the Automatic Procedure) in alternative to the one described in the preceding paragraph. According to CVM Resolution No. 160/22, public offers realized through the Automatic

Procedure are exempted from the need for preliminary analysis of the CVM and can access an unlimited number of potential investors.

XI. The Prospectus

46. Article 16 of CVM Resolution No. 160/22 states that the prospectus must be prepared by the issuer in conjunction with the lead coordinator and contain necessary, sufficient, truthful, accurate, consistent, and up-to-date information, presented in a clear and concise manner, so that investors can make an informed investment decision. Article 84 of the BCA establishes that the prospectus shall clearly and precisely mention the forecasts as to the success of the future enterprise. Accordingly, the prospectus must specifically indicate:

- the capital stock to be subscribed, how it is to be paid up, and whether or not there is authorization for its further increases up to a determined maximum without need for shareholders' meeting approval (authorized capital – *see* paragraph 34);
- the portion of the capital to be paid up in goods (not currency), the description of such goods, and the value ascribed to them;
- the number, types, and classes of shares (*see* paragraphs 34–43 above), their par value (if applicable), and subscription price;
- the amount to be paid up at the time of subscription;
- the liabilities undertaken by the incorporators, the contracts executed on behalf of the future corporation, and the amounts already expended and to be expended;
- the particular benefits to be granted to the incorporators and third parties and the provisions of the draft by-laws in which such benefits are regulated;
- the obtaining of governmental authorization for the incorporation of the company, if applicable;
- the date of beginning of subscription and its closing dates, as well as the financial institution that is authorized to receive the respective payments;
- the solution to be adopted with respect to the amounts received that exceed the value of subscription;
- the term within which the incorporation meeting, or the preliminary meeting for the appraisal of goods paid as capital, shall occur, if that is the case;
- name, nationality, marital status (single, married, divorced, etc.), occupation, and residence of the incorporators, or, in the case of legal entities, its name, nationality, and headquarters, as well as the number and types of shares that each incorporator has subscribed; and
- the financial institution serving as an intermediary of the issuance, where the originals of the prospectus and of the draft by-laws will be deposited, so that any interested person may examine them.

XII. Negotiation with Shares of Its Own Issuance

47. Article 30 of the BCA prevents a corporation from negotiating shares of its own issuance. This restriction has the following exceptions: (a) redemption, refund or amortization transactions provided for by law; (b) shares acquired to be held in the corporation's treasury or cancelled, limited to the amount of the balance of profits or reserves, except the legal reserve, and which may not reduce the corporate capital or shares acquired by donation; (c) the sale of shares acquired under item (b) above, and held in the corporation's treasury; and (d) the purchase of shares upon reduction of capital with restitution of their value to shareholders in cash, provided the market price of the shares is lower or equal to the value to be returned to shareholders.

The acquisition by the corporation of its own shares can take place by means of donation or purchase with any positive value in the accumulated profits account, as long as the capital stock is not reduced.

With respect to publicly held corporations, such acquisition of shares by the issuer itself can happen when a reduction of the company's capital by means of restitution of money to shareholders is resolved, provided that the market price of the shares in the stock exchanges is lower or equal to the value to be refunded to the shareholders for each share. This rule will allow the acquisition of the shares representing the capital to be reduced whenever this is more advantageous for the company than the formal reduction of its capital. Therefore, in this situation, the easiest (and possibly least costly) resource of buying an equity in the market will be allowed. The shares so acquired by the corporation in order to implement the reduction of its outstanding capital are to be permanently taken out of circulation. Thus, they cannot be resold by the company. The acquisition of its own shares by a publicly held corporation shall also comply with the rules established by the CVM, which may subject the validity of such acquisitions to its previous approval.

The reason for such restrictions lies in the fact that a corporation's acquisition of its own shares has the effect of distorting its share capital, which will stop representing money entries from external shareholders. Shares acquired to be held in the corporation's treasury do not grant dividends and voting rights.

XIII. Redemption and Amortization

48. Article 44 of BCA determines that the by-laws or the general shareholders' meeting may authorize the employment of profits or capital surpluses in the redemption or amortization of shares.

Through redemption, the company makes a payment to its shareholders and regains control of shares issued by the company itself. It can happen either by proportionally reducing the capital stock, that is, by cancelling shares, or not. If the shares issued bear a par value, then when they are to be redeemed without a proportional reduction of the corporation's capital stock, such a par value is to be increased accordingly. Except if otherwise established in the company's by-laws, redemption may only take place if approved specifically in a meeting of shareholders entitled to shares representing at least 50% of the class of shares to be affected.

The amortization is the distribution to the shareholders, as an advance, of funds representing the company's net worth that would be payable in case of the corporation's liquidation but without reduction of the capital *stock*. The repayment of the value of the shares may represent the whole or part of their net worth and may be offered to owners of all shares or only to a specific class of them. In case amortization is offered in relation to a part of a specific class of shares only, such part will be selected through the casting of lots.

In accordance with the preceding paragraph, it is possible that shares in a corporation be subject to full amortization. In this case, the shares will be replaced by fruitive shares (*see* paragraph 41 above), the rights of which may suffer restrictions established in the by-laws or by the general shareholders' meeting that established the amortization. It should be stressed that such restrictions shall not be related to the shareholders' essential rights, as per paragraph 74 below.

In the event that a corporation's liquidation takes place, previously to the distribution of the net assets to the shareholders, the shares that have not undergone amortization are to be paid an amount equivalent to that already paid to shares that have undergone amortization, duly corrected according to the rate of inflation. Only after that equalization will the previously amortized shares be allowed to participate in the distribution of the corporation's remaining assets (Article 44, fifth paragraph, of the BCA).

XIV. Repayment

49. Repayment is the transaction according to which the corporation pays the value of its shares to shareholders who dissent from decisions of the general shareholders' meetings in cases permitted by law (Article 45 of the BCA), provided that such shareholders manifest, within thirty days from the date on which the resolution in question is published, their intention to leave (Article 137 of the BCA). The decisions generating such right of withdrawal in favour of dissenting shareholders are the following (Articles 136 and 137 of the BCA):

(1) creation of preferred shares or the increase of an already existing class without proportional increase in the other classes, unless such transactions were already permitted in the by-laws;
(2) modification of the benefits, or of the conditions under which redemptions or amortizations of one or more classes of preferred shares are to be effected, or the creation of a class of preferred shares more favoured than those already existing;
(3) reduction of the minimum mandatory dividend;
(4) merger of the corporation into another company or consolidation of it with another company;
(5) participation in a group of companies;
(6) changing the corporate purpose; and
(7) spin-off of the corporation.

In the cases under items (1) and (2) above, only the shareholders of the types and classes of shares that were negatively affected shall have the right to withdraw from the corporation (Article 137, item I, of the BCA) and in the cases of items (4) and (5) above, the holders of shares of a class or type that has market liquidity and dispersion shall not have the right to withdraw, provided that: (a) liquidity is evidenced when the type or class of share, or the certificate that represents it, is part of a general index representing a portfolio of securities in Brazil or abroad, defined by the CVM; and (b) dispersion is evidenced when the majority shareholder, the controlling corporation or other corporations under their control hold less than half of issued shares of the applicable type or class (Article 137, item II, sub-items (a) and (b), of the BCA). Furthermore, in the case of item (7) above, there shall only be a right to withdraw if the spin-off results in: (a) a change in the corporate purpose, except when the spun-off company is transferred to a corporation with a main line of business that coincides with the line of business of the spun-off company; or (b) a reduction in the mandatory dividend, or (c) participation in a group of companies (Article 137, item III, sub-items (a), (b), and (c), of the BCA).

The value to be paid to the dissenting shareholders may be calculated in accordance with special rules that may be set forth in the by-laws, provided that such value (i) is proportionally equal to or higher than the corporation's net worth indicated in the last balance sheet approved by the general shareholders' meeting, or (ii) is based on the economic value of the shares (Article 45, first paragraph, of the BCA).

The second paragraph of Article 45 of the BCA determines that if the dissenting resolution has been adopted after sixty days from the presentation of the last approved balance sheet, the dissenting shareholder may ask for the preparation of a special balance sheet in order for the net worth to reflect a more realistic value.

In case the repayment is made with proceeds originating from profits or capital surpluses, the repaid shares will be kept by the company. However, in the event that the capital itself is utilized for the repayment, if the repaid shares are not resold within 120 days, the capital is to be reduced accordingly (Article 45, fifth and sixth paragraphs of the BCA).

XV. Debentures

A. *Introduction*

50. Debentures are bonds that grant to third parties who acquire them – not necessarily shareholders – rights of credit against the issuing corporation in accordance with the terms, conditions and maturity indicated in the respective debenture certificate and issuance deed (*see* paragraph 51 below).

The corporation may simultaneously perform more than one issuance of debentures. Also, each issuance may be divided into series. The debentures of the same series must be issued at the same face value and confer equal rights to all of its subscribers (Article 53 of the BCA).

B. Issuance Deed

51. The issuance deed is the instrument wherein the corporation indicates the rights conferred upon the debenture holders, their guarantees, if any, and all other terms and conditions applicable to the issuance (Article 61 of the BCA). The issuance deed must be amended for each new series of debentures issued.

The term deed is usually only adopted in Brazil for public instruments drafted and executed before a notary public, although literally, it means written instruments of any kind.

Article 52 of the BCA does not make specific mention of a 'public' or 'private' deed. However, the first paragraph of Article 61 of the BCA expressly acknowledges that such deed may be either public or private. Both 'public' or 'private' issuance deeds shall be filed with the commercial register in order for the issuance to be valid (Article 62, item I, of the BCA).

The issuance deed of debentures to be publicly traded must also be executed by the fiduciary agent of the holders (*see* paragraph 61 below). Still, with respect to publicly traded debentures, the CVM is authorized to establish standard clauses and conditions to be adopted in the issuance deed and to deny any public distribution that does not follow such standards (Article 61, third paragraph of the BCA).

C. Indexing

52. Article 54, first paragraph, of the BCA expressly authorizes debentures to carry monetary, exchange rate (in the specific cases permitted by law), or other type of indexing not forbidden by law.

D. Maturity

53. It is permitted for a corporation to issue debentures without maturity date, such maturity to take place only if interests fail to be paid or if the corporation is dissolved, or in case another previously established condition occurs (Article 55, third paragraph, of the BCA).

E. Interest

54. A debenture may entitle its owner to a fixed or variable rate of interest, participation in the profits of the corporation and a refund premium (Article 56 of the BCA).

F. Convertibility into Shares

55. Additionally, debentures may, under the conditions contained in its issuance deed, be convertible into shares of the issuer (Article 57 of the BCA). For that purpose, the issuance deed must specify:

- the number of shares into which each debenture may be converted or the relation to be adopted between the debentures' face value and the subscription price of the shares;
- the types and classes of the shares into which the debentures may be converted;
- the term within which the debenture holder may apply for the conversion; and
- any other conditions to which the issuance may be subject.

The shareholders have a right of first refusal in the subscription of debentures convertible into shares, to be regulated by the same provisions applicable to the right of first refusal in the subscription of capital increases (*see* paragraph 35 above – Article 57, first paragraph, of the BCA).

Any amendment to the by-laws of a corporation issuing debentures convertible into shares will depend on the approval of the debentures' holders through a resolution in a special meeting of debenture holders or on the approval of their fiduciary agent, if the amendment refers to the following subjects (Article 57, second paragraph, of the BCA): (i) modification of the corporate purposes; or (ii) creation of preferences or modification of existing preferences, if such creation or modification will negatively interfere with the rights of the holders of the shares into which the debentures may be converted.

G. Charges Guaranteeing Debentures

56. Debentures may be guaranteed by charges on specific items of real estate or chattels of the issuing company or by floating charges (preferred right over non-preferred creditors with respect to the corporation's assets in relation to other preferred creditors) or may not be guaranteed at all – in such case granting their holder the status of a non-preferred creditor. Finally, the credits in a debenture may still be subordinated to the non-preferred creditors (Article 58 of the BCA).

Charges on real estate and chattels and floating charges may be cumulative (Article 58, second paragraph, of the BCA). Among debentures with floating charges, the holders of more recent issuances are preferred. Within the same issuance, however, holders of different classes are concurrent (Article 58, third paragraph, of the BCA).

As to charges on real estate, the issuance deed shall be filed with the competent real estate public registry for the guarantee to be valid before third parties (Article 58, fifth paragraph, of the BCA).

If the issuing corporation participates in a group of companies as defined in paragraph 105 below, the debentures may bear a floating guarantee granted by two or more companies of that group (Article 58, sixth paragraph, of the BCA).

H. Amount

57. In the past, debentures were issued according to the limits imposed by Article 60 of the BCA. However, Law No. 12431, dated 27 June 2011, revoked such Article, and no limitations currently exist.

I. Shareholder Approval

58. The issuance of debentures must be approved by the general shareholders' meeting in terms of Article 59 of the BCA. In accordance with the by-laws, the general shareholders' meeting shall state: (i) the amount of the issuance or the criteria to establish its limit and its division into series, if any; (ii) the number and par value of the debentures; (iii) the guarantees in rem or floating charge, if any; (iv) the monetary adjustment conditions, if any; (v) whether or not the debentures are convertible into shares and the conditions of such conversion; (vi) the time and conditions of maturity, amortization or redemption; (vii) the time and conditions of payment of interest, participation in profits and refund premiums, if any; and (viii) the method of subscription or placement and the type of debentures.

In publicly held corporations, the Board of Directors may decide on the issuance of non-convertible debentures, except if otherwise provided for in the corporation's by-laws. Moreover, the by-laws of publicly held corporations may authorize the Board of Directors to, within the limit of the authorized capital, decide on the issuance of debentures convertible into shares, specifying the limit of the capital increase resulting from the conversion of debentures, such limit defined as an amount of capital or in number of shares, and the types and classes of shares that may be issued.

J. Form

59. Originally, debentures could either be issued to the bearer or subject to endorsement. However, as per paragraph 42 above, Law No. 8021, dated 12 April 1990, abolished securities issued to the bearer. In view of that, debentures must now be issued in nominative form, and endorsements must identify the endorsee. The transfers of endorsable debentures are to be registered in a special book maintained by the issuing corporation (Article 63 of the BCA).

K. Modifications

60. After an issuance of debentures is made, any modification of their conditions must be approved by a joint meeting of the holders of securities under that specific issuance and series (*see* paragraph 62 below). The issuance deed must establish the quorum necessary for the approval of the modification in the meeting of debenture holders, provided that such quorum does not represent less than one-half of the outstanding debentures (Article 71, fifth paragraph, of the BCA).

L. Fiduciary Agent

61. Until the enactment of the BCA, the general meeting of debenture holders was the only body able to represent the debenture holders as a group before the issuing corporation. The position of fiduciary agent was then created by the BCA, to be undertaken by a person representing all debenture holders before the issuing corporation, in accordance with the terms of the issuance deed (Article 68 of the BCA).

The fiduciary agent will be permanently in charge of supervising the business and administration of the corporation on behalf of the debenture holders.

The participation of a fiduciary agent on behalf of the debenture holders is mandatory exclusively when the debentures in question are to be publicly traded. Otherwise, the existence of such an agent is optional. The following are the fiduciary agent's duties (Article 68, first paragraph, of the BCA):

- to protect the debenture holders' rights and interests, for which purpose he must employ the same care and zeal that any active and honest man would employ in the administration of his/her own interests and business;
- to prepare and present to the debenture holders yearly, within four months from the closing of the corporation's tax year, a report on all relevant facts occurred during that year that may potentially affect the fulfilment of obligations embodied in the debentures or related to the guarantee of the issuance; and
- within the maximum term of sixty days, give notice to the debenture holders of any default by the corporation in the obligations undertaken in the issuance deed.

The issuance deed may impose additional duties on the fiduciary agent, such as the authentication of debenture certificates, keeping deposits of assets pledged as security, and paying interests, amortizations, and redemptions (Article 69 of the BCA).

The fiduciary agent is not qualified to decide on amendments to the issuance deed. However, in order to effectively protect the rights of the debenture holders, the fiduciary agent may employ any legal action. Specifically, in the case of default of the issuer, he/she/it may (Article 68, third paragraph, of the BCA):

- declare the debentures matured in advance and proceed with the respective collection in accordance with the terms of the issuance deed;
- promote the foreclosure of any guarantees constituted on real estate or chattels;
- file a petition for winding up of the company;
- represent the debenture holders in the issuer's winding up settlement with creditors or non-judicial intervention or liquidation, unless the general meeting of debenture holders resolves to the contrary; and
- take any other necessary steps to ensure the payment of the credits of the debenture holders.

The appointment of the fiduciary agent, as well as acceptance of that duty, are to be effected in the issuance deed (Article 66 of the BCA), which must also indicate the remuneration and the conditions for replacement of the agent, whenever necessary (Article 67 of the BCA).

Only individuals who satisfy the requirements of holding office in a corporation's administrative body and financial institutions that have been specially authorized by the Central Bank of Brazil for the purpose of the administration or custody of third party's assets may be appointed as fiduciary agents (Article 66, first paragraph, of the BCA). As far as publicly traded debentures are concerned, only the latter may be appointed (CVM Resolution No. 17, dated February 9 2021).

M. General Meeting of Debenture Holders

62. The holders of debentures of the same issuance and series may at any time gather in a general meeting for the purpose of resolving any matters of their common interest (Article 71 of the BCA). The fiduciary agent shall always be present at that general meeting and must disclose to the holders any pertinent information requested. The general meeting of debenture holders may be called by the fiduciary agent, by the issuing corporation, by holders representing at least 10% of the outstanding debentures, or by the CVM (Article 71, first paragraph, of the BCA). The meeting will follow the same procedures established for general meetings of shareholders when applicable.

N. Issuance Abroad

63. Article 73 of the BCA states that only upon previous approval by the Central Bank of Brazil may the Brazilian corporation issue debentures abroad guaranteed by assets located in Brazilian territory. That means that a Brazilian corporation may at any time issue debentures abroad without need for any governmental authorization if said debentures are not guaranteed by assets within Brazil.

If the corporation issues debentures abroad with floating or real charges on assets located in Brazilian territory, the guarantee clause will be deemed null and therefore not capable of foreclosure in favour of the creditors.

Such rule reflects the traditional aim of protecting the country's economy by avoiding the flow of assets abroad without reasonable compensation. It is introduced in order for the Central Bank of Brazil to verify whether the amount of the issuance guaranteed is not smaller in value than the assets to be foreclosed in case the guarantee has to be made effective.

Under the same rationale, the first paragraph of Article 73 of the BCA establishes, specifically with respect to foreign companies authorized to do business in Brazil, that Brazilian creditors shall be preferred over creditors of debentures issued abroad, unless the issuance abroad has been previously authorized by the Central Bank of Brazil and the proceeds of the issuance have been fully invested in the country. The preference of Brazilian creditors over foreigners concerns only assets located in the country.

In addition to verifying the fairness of the consideration received by the Brazilian issuer in the event of foreclosure of the guarantees, the Central Bank of Brazil shall ascertain whether the remuneration of the debentures is in accordance with market conditions. Accordingly, the second paragraph of Article 73 of the BCA states that only the principal and interest on debentures registered with the Central Bank of Brazil will be remitted abroad. These provisions have to be construed in light of Law No. 14286, dated 29 December 2021 and its administrative regulation by the Central Bank of Brazil. Said law regulates the Brazilian foreign exchange market and the flow of capital in and out of Brazil.

According to Law No. 14286/21 and Central Bank of Brazil Resolution No. 278, dated 31 December 2022, the raising of capital through the issue of debentures abroad, in a value equal to or higher than US$ 1 million, requires, rather than registration, the supplying to the Central Bank of Brazil of information on the issue of debentures, its value, payment conditions and time of payment.

It should be stressed that the acquisition and sale of foreign currency within the Brazilian territory linked to the disbursement and/or repayment of principal and interest on debentures must necessarily have a financial institution as a party.

As to any debentures issued abroad, either by Brazilian corporations or by foreign entities, their negotiation within the Brazilian capital market will depend on the previous approval by the CVM.

XVI. Subscription Bonds

64. The corporation may issue bonds granting to their holders the right to subscribe shares according to the terms and conditions expressed in the certificate of the bonds (Article 75 of the BCA). Such subscription bonds may either be sold by the corporation or conferred as an additional benefit to those who subscribe to shares or debentures of its issuance (Article 77 of the BCA).

The amount of capital that may be increased by means of the exercising of all subscription rights within subscription bonds is limited to the amount of the authorized capital (Article 75 of the BCA). This means that subscription bonds must be issued in accordance with the limit within which the administrators of the corporation may increase the capital without approval by the general shareholders' meeting.

The power to resolve the issuance of subscription bonds is granted by the BCA to the general shareholders' meeting, but the corporation's by-laws may instead bestow such powers on the Board of Directors (Article 76 of the BCA). As per the pre-emptive right in the case of subscription of shares, the shareholders of the corporation are also granted preference on the acquisition of subscription bonds (*see* paragraph 35 above – Article 77, sole paragraph, of the BCA).

§3. Shareholders, Management, and Control

I. Introduction: Structural and Administrative Bodies

65. The management of Brazilian corporations is structurally divided into four bodies: the general meeting of shareholders, the Board of Directors, the Board of Officers, and the Board of Auditors. The main legal provisions and rules pertaining to such bodies will be focused on below.

II. The General Meeting of Shareholders

A. *Attributions*

66. The general meeting of shareholders is hierarchically the first body of the Brazilian corporation. It is empowered to decide all matters related to the attainment of a company's purpose, pursuant to Article 121 of the BCA. The wide drafting of such provision obviously has the scope of granting the general meeting broad powers to deliberate on any matters relating to the company. Some of the general meeting's deliberative functions are exclusively attributed to such body (Article 122 of the BCA). They are the following:

- amend the corporate by-laws;
- elect and dismiss administrators and auditors, except officers, when the company has a board of directors;
- approve the accounts presented by the administrators;
- authorize the issuance of debentures and profit participation bonds;
- suspend the rights of any shareholder based on breach of his/her obligations under the by-laws and applicable statutes;
- approve the valuation of any goods to be incorporated in the capital stock of the company;
- approve the merger, spin-off and winding up of the company, as well as the change in its corporate type; and
- authorize the administrators to file a petition for the winding up of the company or for a judicial settlement with creditors.

B. *Ordinary and Extraordinary General Meetings of Shareholders and Their Quorum Requirements*

67. There are two kinds of general meetings, according to the BCA. The difference between them is related to the issues they address. In terms of Article 132, ordinary general meetings have exclusive authority to: (i) examine the accounts of the administrators and the financial statements of the company; (ii) deliberate on the destination to be given to the profits of the previous years and declare the payment of dividends; and (iii) elect the administrators and the members of the Board of Auditors. Extraordinary general meetings of shareholders have authority to deliberate on any other issue.

Ordinary general meetings are to be held at least once a year before the last day of the fourth month, subsequent to the end of each fiscal year. In this regard, it is different from the extraordinary general meetings of shareholders. The law does not stipulate a fixed time for the convening of such later meetings, stating only that they must be held whenever any deliberation not included among those for which an ordinary meeting is required is to be taken. In substance, there is no procedural difference between ordinary and extraordinary meetings of shareholders.

Materially, the main difference between the two kinds of general meetings, apart from the subjects that may be dealt with within each of them, is the minimum quorum required for decisions. There are two types of quorums to be considered. The first is the quorum for regular installation of a general shareholders' meeting. Such is obtained, as a general rule, if shareholders representing one-quarter of the total votes granted by shares with voting rights are present at any meeting (Article 125 of the BCA). In case, however, such quorum is not attained, a second meeting can be convened and installed with any quorum.

Such rule is generally valid for ordinary general meetings but is subject to severe qualifications in case of extraordinary general meetings. These, in case their purpose is the introduction of any amendment to the by-laws of the company, must be installed with a minimum quorum of shareholders representing two-thirds of the total votes granted by shares with voting rights in the first meeting convened. If such quorum cannot be obtained, a second meeting may be convened and installed free from quorum requirements (Article 135 of the BCA). A second form of quorum has, however, been created by the law in relation to extraordinary general meetings. This is a quorum for valid deliberation, requiring a minimum number of shareholders' votes for certain decisions in order to prevent deliberations affecting members' rights or the conditions under which they accepted to take part in a venture be changed without their material consent.

In this sense, Article 136 of the BCA establishes that shareholders representing at least 50% of the total votes granted by shares with voting rights must vote in favour of any general meeting resolution concerning the following topics, except if a greater quorum is required by the company's by-laws:

- creation of preferred shares, or increase in the number of already existing shares of a class, out of proportion with increase in other classes, unless this is expressly authorized in the by-laws;
- amendment in the preferences, advantages or rights attributed to any class of shares or creation of a new class of shares;
- reduction in the minimum dividend to be paid yearly to shareholders;
- merger of the company with another corporation or its consolidation;
- integration of the company into a group of companies;
- change in the purposes of the company;
- end of the state of liquidation of the company;
- creation of profit participation bonds;
- spin-off of the company; and
- voluntary winding up of the company.

A further protection is granted to preferential shareholders by Article 136, first paragraph of the BCA, which requires that any measures taken in accordance with items (i) and (ii) of the previous paragraph be also approved by members holding more than half of each class of preferred shares affected, in a special meeting called by the officers of the corporation and held according to the formalities set forth in the BCA.

C. Convening of Meetings and the Principle of Disclosure

68. The rules concerning the form for convening meetings implement the principle of full disclosure, which has a strong influence on company law worldwide. Normally, the general meetings are to be convened by the Board of Directors, if existent, or by the officers. As in many other jurisdictions, it is possible for the Board of Auditors or for the members of the company to convene a shareholders' meeting. In terms of Article 123, sole paragraph, item 'b' of the BCA, any shareholder may convene a meeting if the administrators of the company fail to call it within sixty days from the date it becomes necessary. Besides, members holding 5% or more of the capital stock may petition the administration to call a meeting, and if the request is not attended to within eight days, the members can themselves convene the meeting. Also, members holding 5% or more of the voting capital or 5% or more of the non-voting capital may call a meeting if the administration fails to call a meeting within eight days of the request for the election of the Board of Auditors (Article 123 of the BCA). Formally, a general meeting of shareholders, either ordinary or extraordinary, is to be convened through notices published three times both in a newspaper of wide circulation and in the government's official gazette (Article 124 of the BCA). In privately held corporations, the general meeting of shareholders must not take place before eight days have elapsed from the first publication of the notice. In case the meeting has to be convened a second time, for example, for lack of quorum, the same notice requirements will be applicable, with the difference that the meeting must not be held before five days have elapsed from the first republication of the notice, in case of privately held corporations. As to publicly held corporations, such periods are fifteen and eight days, respectively. At any rate, the traditional Roman-law principle that substance must prevail over form will be applicable here, since any irregularity in the convening of a meeting will be disregarded if all shareholders are present.

Specifically in relation to ordinary general meetings, Article 133 of the BCA adds a formality to their convening. It states that they must be preceded by the placing of the financial statements, the report of the administration, the report of the Board of Auditors, and any other relevant documents at the disposal of the members at least one month prior to the date the meeting is held.

At this point, it must be stressed that a frequent contention in litigation involving a company and/or its members is based on the invalidity of general meetings of shareholders due to procedural irregularities. In spite of its controversial nature in civil-law systems, case law shows that it is a firm proposition that they can be declared void.

With regard to publicly held corporations, CVM Resolution No. 81, dated 29 March 2022, sets forth specific requirements for information disclosure that shall be observed by the company and its managers when calling a general meeting of shareholders. Such requirements are tailored to the matters to be submitted to the shareholders in the relevant general meeting.

D. The Proxy Machinery

69. Article 126, first paragraph, of the BCA, provides that shareholders may vote in general meetings through duly appointed proxies. CVM Resolution No. 81/22 also establishes relevant rules applicable to the appointment of proxies by shareholders of publicly held corporations. The proxy must himself be an administrator of the company, another shareholder or a lawyer. In case of publicly held corporations, the proxy may also be a financial institution such as a commercial or investment bank. This last extension of the rule has been noted upon the entering into force of the BCA as a strategic effort to stimulate the concentration of shareholdings in the hands of financial institutions in order to favour the formation of large economic groups headed by them.

The soliciting of proxies as a means of obtaining control of a corporation has turned into a widespread practice in many countries, but only recently has it been turning into a common practice in Brazil. This is due to the fact that Brazilian companies tended to be family-owned and thus under majority control, but with the increase of the initial public offers in the last years, this scenario is changing. At any rate, the BCA (Article 126, second paragraph) contains rather detailed rules designed to avoid abuses in obtaining proxies. According to such rules, all requests for proxies must: (i) contain complete information on the way the voting rights requested will be exercised; (ii) enable the shareholder to nominate another proxy at any time in case he afterwards decides to vote differently; and must also (iii) be addressed to all shareholders whose addresses are available in the company. Furthermore, in case of publicly held corporations, the proxies must be restricted to only one general meeting (Article 52, item III, of the CVM Resolution No. 81/22).

Besides, any shareholder or group of shareholders representing 0.5% of the capital is entitled to receive from the company, upon request, a list of the shareholders to which proxy proposals have been sent (Article 126, third paragraph, of the BCA and Article 58 of the CVM Resolution No. 81/22).[15] With regard to the mentioned list of shareholders, in accordance with CVM Resolution No. 81/22, the company is not allowed to (i) require any justification for supplying the list; (ii) charge for the provision of the list; or (iii) subject the provision of the list to the accomplishment of any formalities or the presentation of any documents not provided for in Article 126, second paragraph, of the BCA.

It must also be stressed that according to Article 56 of CVM Resolution No. 81/22, in the event that proxies are requested for appointing members of the board of directors or of the board of auditors of a publicly held corporation, shareholders representing at least 0.5% of the capital may indicate other individuals to be included in the relevant proxy as candidates to hold offices in the company's administrative bodies. Additionally, the company is required to reimburse certain expenses incurred in connection with the proxies' requests of shareholders representing a portion equal to or greater than 0.5% of the capital, unless it maintains an electronic system of placement of proxies' requests over the Internet (Article 60 of the CVM Resolution No. 81/22).

---

15. In this sense please refer to Modesto Carvalhosa, *A Nova Lei das Sociedades Anônimas – Seu Modelo Econômico*, 2nd edn (Editora Paz e Terra, 1977), 102 ff., Rio de Janeiro.

III. Shareholders' Rights in General

70. We must now focus on the rights of majority and minority shareholders. Those of the majority obviously receive shorter statutory treatment than those relating to the minority. As an introduction to the topic, it must be said that, as a general rule, the common-law principle that the court shall not interfere with the internal affairs of a company, unless oppression of the minority or gross irregularities are shown, is entirely applicable in Brazil.

A. Rights of the Majority Towards the Minority

71. The main way through which the rights of the majority may be impaired by the minority is through the emulative or wrongful employment of the latter's voting rights. Actually, a hostile minority may damage the affairs of a company by raising irrelevant suspicions and incidents in general meetings. Such strategies may impair the company's public image or credit and even create administrative problems. The BCA seeks to prevent such abuses by imposing on all shareholders a duty to use their voting rights exclusively in the interests of the company (Article 115 of the BCA). Votes cast with the intention of causing unlawful damage to the corporation or to other shareholders are also forbidden. The same is applicable to votes cast in situations of conflict of interest between shareholder and company. The penalty for violation is liability for damages, and it is applicable even in case the liable shareholder has been outvoted (Article 115, third paragraph of the BCA).

B. Rights and Protection of the Minority

72. The statute understandably pays extra attention to the provision of protection of the minority, given the risk of oppression by controlling shareholders. The protection statutorily granted to minority shareholders encompasses both generic and specific provisions.

a. General protection of the minority

73. The generic provisions are those protecting the minority through the imposition of liability on controlling shareholders for oppressive conduct described in fairly general terms. In this sense, Article 115 of the BCA declares as oppressive conduct generating liability for controlling shareholders any acts or policies adopted by a company to the detriment of its shareholders. Article 117 of the BCA lists such acts as ultra vires acts or transactions not at arm's length favouring other companies, especially other companies of the same economic group. The rule also encompasses the adoption of any policies or practices that are detrimental to the company under the influence of a controlling shareholder. Among such practices and policies, we can point out the election of an inept administrator or the entering by controlling shareholders into favoured transactions with the controlled company. For the purpose of applying the above-mentioned rules, the concept of a controlling shareholder is detailed in a somewhat enigmatic fashion in Article 116 of the BCA. In terms of such provision, a controlling shareholder may be an individual, a legal entity or a group of individuals and/or legal entities linked by a voting agreement or unified control that detains voting rights capable of warranting the permanent majority in general meetings and electing the majority of the administrators. Besides the effective use of the controlling power, there is also a requirement for the qualification as a controlling shareholder. This has been the object of an extensive academic discussion as to its meaning, since, literally interpreted, it might exclude silent majority shareholders from liability. This would be especially unfair in cases in which a minority shareholder benefits from the omission to effectively control the company, since this latter minority shareholder would not pass the test of having enough voting rights and thus would not be considered a controlling shareholder. The consequence would be the creation of a vacuum in regard to liability, which would be likely to stimulate the oppression of the minority. Various solutions have been devised to deal with this problem. Among these, some maintain that the requirement as to effective control would apply only to legal entities as opposed to individuals. For others, the provision must be interpreted strictly, whatever its undesirable effects. The view favoured by us, however, is that the majority shareholder who does not use his/her/its power is indirectly acting if he/she/it effectively voluntarily relinquishes the control to others. Thus, he/she/it should suffer the burden of liability. In a final vote about the topic, it must be stressed that Article 116 of the BCA is wide enough to cover minority control.

b. Specific protection of the minority: essential and non-essential rights

74. The minority is also protected through the attribution of rights specifically described in the legislation. Such rights are considered essential whenever they grant shareholders a prerogative that is deemed by the law to be central to the notion of shareholder/partner and that cannot be excluded by the provisions in the by-laws or in any documents filed in a company's incorporation. Such rights are listed in Article 109 of the BCA and include the following: (i) to participate in the profits; (ii) to participate in the distribution of the net assets of the company in case of winding up; (iii) to supervise the administration of the business of the company; (iv) to be granted preference in the acquisition of securities issued (shares, convertible debentures, subscription bonuses); and (v) to withdraw from the corporation in the cases prescribed by the law.

The right to participate in the distribution of profits has two main aspects. The first is that it cannot be excluded in relation to any member, since it is essential to the concept of shareholder. Besides, such right is quantified through the imposition of a minimum dividend to be declared annually by the administration of the company. If the by-laws are silent, the minimum dividend will correspond to 50% of the yearly profits after the deduction of certain reserves, a percentage that can be reduced to 25% by a provision in the by-laws (Article 202 of the BCA).

The rights referring to the supervision of the company are further specified by provisions granting shareholders representing at least 5% of the capital a right to require before the court the exhibition of the accounting books of the corporation in case a suspicion of violation of the law or of the by-laws of the company can be entertained (Article 105 of the BCA). Another instance of the same right of supervision is given by Article 141 of the BCA, under the terms of which shareholders representing 10% of the voting capital may require cumulative voting for the election of the Board of Directors, through which the number of votes cast by each share is multiplied by the number of positions to be filled. This procedure, which is very well known in the US, tends to render the election of a representative of the minority for the Board easier, the functions of which include the supervision of the corporation's administration.

Another very important essential right is the possibility of withdrawing from the company in case basic characteristics of the business or the way it is conducted are altered. This rests in civil-law countries like Brazil, where the theoretical consideration is that corporations are based upon a contract. One consequence of such consideration is the requirement to provide the shareholders (deemed as 'parties' to such theoretical contract) with enough flexibility to withdraw in case any of the substantial conditions of the association are changed. The changes giving rise to a right of withdrawal are indicated in paragraph 49 above.

Apart from that, shareholders representing at least 5% of a privately held corporation may also apply in court for withdrawal in case they deem the corporation unable to meet its purposes (Article 599, second paragraph of the Brazilian Civil Procedure Code). Such inability to meet purposes may arise in case of conflict among members, objective economic difficulties and other causes.

The list contained in Article 109 of the BCA, however, does not embody all the rights of the members of a corporation that cannot be excluded by specific provisions in the by-laws and other documents filed upon a company's incorporation. Other essential rights of a member not included in Article 109 of the BCA are:

- the right of the holders of voting shares in a publicly held corporation to fair treatment upon the transfer of control of a company ensured through the obligatory presentation of a tender offer by the acquirer for at least 80% of the amount paid for the voting shares comprising the controlling block (Article 254-A of the BCA);
- the right to negotiate shares freely, in spite of the fact that minor limitations such as a pre-emptive right in favour of other shareholders may be imposed by the by-laws (Article 36 of the BCA);
- the right of non-voting shareholders to take part in general meetings and participate in the discussion of the topics to be voted on in such meetings (Article 125, sole paragraph, of the BCA); and
- many procedural rights to be exercised during general meetings of a company with the objective of granting full disclosure and information on the matters treated therein.

Besides the rights discussed above, others are granted to the general body of shareholders or to some of them; some of such rights, however, are subject to exclusion through specific provisions in the by-laws or documents filed upon the incorporation of the company. These are the non-essential shareholders' rights and the most important of such class of rights is the vote.

As a general rule, all shares have one voting right unless the by-laws state the contrary. However, the by-laws may exclude the voting rights in preferred shares under the terms of Article 111 of the BCA (*see* paragraph 39 above). This exclusion will be limited to a maximum of 50% of the whole capital of the company (Article 15, second paragraph, of the BCA – *see* paragraph 39 above).

Apart from the vote, the list of shareholders' rights that may be excluded by provisions in the by-laws is extremely wide. Since private law and thus the law of corporations is governed by the 'waivable rights' principle, it must be accepted as a rule that all rights are capable of being excluded if the general meeting of shareholders so determines, unless there is any express or implied provision to the contrary. Nevertheless, it will always be possible for the affected members to oppose the exclusion of their rights, based on the above-mentioned provisions imposing liability on majority shareholders in case oppression of the minority can be shown.

IV. Officers and Board of Directors

A. *General Considerations*

75. Below the general meeting of shareholders, the law places the two administrative bodies: the Board of Directors and the officers. These tend to be regulated by many fixed rules, which cannot be changed by provisions that are contrary to the by-laws. This intention to endow corporations with a fixed administrative structure can be seen as a consequence of the institutionalist approach to corporations that characterizes the Brazilian legal system. Both members of the Board of Directors and officers are considered administrators in terms of the BCA.

B. *The Board of Directors*

76. The Board of Directors receives detailed legal treatment in Articles 138–142 of the BCA. Its existence is generally unnecessary in privately held corporations. However, the existence of a Board of Directors is mandatory for publicly held corporations, companies with authorized capital and state-controlled corporations.

In the corporations in which a Board of Directors exists, the by-laws must indicate the number of Directors, their term of office and the formalities for their appointment. Mandatory provisions, however, restrict the possibility of choice. The first is that the Board must have at least three members and that their term of office shall not surpass three years, although their re-election is permitted. It is to be stressed that both the election and dismissal of members of the Board of Directors are deferred to the general meeting of shareholders by the above-mentioned Article 122, item II, of the BCA.

C. *The Officers*

77. The officers are to be elected by the Board of Directors, in case such body exists in the corporation. Otherwise, the officers are to be elected by the general meeting of shareholders under the terms of Article 143 of the BCA. At any rate, the term of office of each officer shall not surpass three years, and re-election is permitted.

D. Requirements for Election of Administrators

78. Both the members of the Board of Directors and the officers must be individuals (Article 146 of the BCA). As provided by Law No. 14195/21, there is no restriction concerning the election of foreign residents as administrators. The refusal of admission of legal entities as officers, features to be found in many foreign jurisdictions, is a distinctive characteristic of Brazilian law.

Members of the Board of Directors and officers residing or domiciled abroad may only be vested in their positions by appointing a representative residing in Brazil, having powers to receive service of process in actions brought against the foreign resident. The appointment is to be done by means of a power of attorney with a validity extending over a period of at least three years after the end of the foreign resident's term in office.

Moreover, all those criminally convicted for the practice of economic crimes or declared barred by the CVM (in relation to the holding of administrative positions in publicly floated companies) cannot be elected as either members of the Board of Directors or officers.

E. Remuneration of Administrators

79. The remuneration of the administrators, including any benefits and allowances, is to be fixed yearly by the general meeting of shareholders, taking into account their professional experience, the market value of their services, their professional duties and reputation (Article 152 of the BCA). Administrators may be admitted to share yearly profits. In terms of Article 152, first paragraph of the BCA, the profits attributed to members of the Board of Directors and to the officers will, at any rate, be limited to: (i) the yearly remuneration of the administrators; or (ii) one-tenth of the yearly profits, whichever is the less.

CVM Resolution No. 80/22 states in its Annex C that publicly held corporations are required to disclose, among other information concerning their administrators' remuneration, the maximum, minimum and average individual remuneration paid in the last three fiscal years for (i) the board of directors; and (ii) the board of officers. Such rule also applies to the Board of Auditors, which is explained below.

F. Term in Office of Administrators

80. The administrators shall leave office upon the expiration of the term for which they have been elected if they are not re-elected or upon their resignation. Moreover, the members of the Board of Directors and officers may be dismissed by the general meeting of shareholders as the sovereign deliberative organ of the Brazilian corporation (Article 122, item II, of the BCA) at any time. The officers may also be dismissed by the Board of Directors (Article 142, item II, of the BCA).

G. The Power and Structure of the Board of Directors and of the Officers

81. As to the powers of the Board of Directors and of the officers, it must be stressed that the BCA states that the administrative attributions assigned by the law to an administrative body cannot be transferred to another through clauses in the by-laws (Article 139 of the BCA).

In order to understand the specific difference between the Board of Directors and the officers, it must be mentioned that the former is normally said to be invested in deliberative functions, whereas the latter is endowed with executive functions. This double administrative structure follows the scheme adopted in the US, which actually inspired the drafting of Brazilian statutes. In fact, the board of officers and executive officers of American companies inspired the creation of the Board of Directors and of the functions of officers in the Brazilian corporation, respectively.

A structural difference accompanies, as always, the functional difference. Such structural difference is that the Board of Directors is a collegiate organ; that is, its decisions are taken on a majority basis, whereas the decisions of the officers are individual within their specific areas of attribution (Articles 140, item IV, and 143 of the BCA). The officers may exceptionally deliberate by majority vote only in connection with matters listed in the by-laws (Article 143, second paragraph, of the BCA).

The diverse legal treatment for the Board of Directors and the officers may be explained on the grounds that the former has been designed as an organ in which the various groups influencing control of a corporation would be present through representatives. Their powers should then be balanced by the majority decision. Because of its collegiate nature, the Board of Directors obviously could not have powers to represent the company. Such powers are in fact incidental to executive functions and are conferred exclusively upon the officers (Article 138, first paragraph of the BCA). To the Board of Directors, the law confers the attribution to fix general guidelines as to the way the business of the corporation is to be conducted (Article 142, item I of the BCA). Besides, it is also empowered to develop supervisory functions, inspect books of the company and even dismiss officers (Article 142, items II, III, and V, of the BCA). A third set of functions is the approval of transactions relevant to the company, such as the sale or imposition of burdens on fixed assets of the company and the entering into contracts deemed relevant by the by-laws (Article 142, items VI and VIII, of the BCA), among other attributions.[16]

16. It must at this point be stressed that such position is not unanimously accepted in Brazilian legal doctrine. It has been argued that both the Board of Directors and the officers perform executive functions, the main difference among them being the fact that only the latter can represent the company (*see* Modesto Carvalhosa, *Comentários à Lei das Sociedades Anônimas*, vol. 5 (São Paulo: Saraiva, 7).

In order to prevent concentration of power and influence over the administrative bodies of publicly held corporations, Law No. 14195/21 introduced the third paragraph to Article 138 of the BCA, prohibiting in their case the accumulation of the positions of Chairman of the Board of Directors and main officer (Chief Executive Officer).

H. Duties of Administrators

a. Fiduciary nature of duties and their judicial enforcement

82. The duties of administrators tend to receive a uniform treatment in Brazilian law, applicable to both officers and members of the Board of Directors. The content of such duties is clearly of a fiduciary nature, which is a consequence of the strong influence of common law upon Brazilian corporation statutes. Such duties are in general owed to the company and not to individual shareholders. This is made plain by the provision that the administrator, even if elected by a separate group or class of shareholders, may not defend their interests by breaching the fiduciary duties owed to the company (Article 154, first paragraph of the BCA). Individual shareholders are also granted rights of action to correct wrongs done to them issued from the conduct of the officers. Damages may in fact be awarded for such wrongs according to the general liability provisions contained in Article 186 of the BCC, according to which those recklessly or wantonly causing damage to others should make good the loss. It is our opinion that there will at any rate be objectionable damages in terms of Article 186 of the BCC whenever any of the fiduciary duties prescribed in the BCA is breached, thereby issuing an economic loss to the shareholders. Such economic loss may be the decrease in the value of the shares. As a result, it can be taken as a conclusion that the duties owed to the company may also create a course of action for the individual shareholder, in case he/she can prove his/her economic loss.

One must note that the shareholder may act against the officer or against the members of the Board of Directors in a derivative capacity in case the damaged company fails to do so within three months after the general meeting of shareholders that deliberated to file a suit for damages against the administrator (Article 159, third paragraph of the BCA). In case the general meeting decides not to file a suit, the damages may be pursued in court by shareholders representing at least 5% of the capital stock on behalf of the company.

b. To whom the duties are owed

83. Besides the company and individual shareholders, fiduciary duties are also owed to the community in general, the administrators of the corporation being compelled by Article 154 of the BCA to act having in view the public interest and the social function of a business enterprise. This is an eloquent example of the effects of the institutional view of the corporation that influenced Brazilian law. Its practical consequence is the possibility of the administrators approving deliberation pursuant to which the companies grant reasonable advantages to the community or to its workers.

c. General standard for measuring liability: duty of care

84. The general standard for measuring liability of the administrators is furnished by Article 153 of the BCA. According to such provision, the administrator of a corporation should perform his/her duties with the care and diligence normally employed by an active and honest individual in the management of his/her own affairs. Such care and diligence must be employed towards furthering the objects of the company, it being forbidden (with the public interest exception above) that administrators grant third parties (including shareholders) any advantage without due consideration (Article 154 and paragraphs of the BCA). The same provision also prevents them from using the corporation's money, credit, services or facilities in general for their private benefit, as well as from accepting remuneration from third parties in connection with activities performed as administrators of the company.

d. Duty to avoid secret profits

85. Stringent prohibitions are also imposed on obtaining secret profits by administrators of a company, according to the terms of Article 155 of the BCA. Pursuant to such prohibitions, administrators may not take private advantage of business opportunities that could be advantageously used by the company. Because of the fiduciary nature of the relationships, this extends to all business advantages, whether or not the knowledge about it was obtained by the administrator acting professionally. The prohibition extends to the acquisition, for later resale at a profit to the corporation, of any goods or raw materials the latter may need.

e. Duty to avoid conflict of interest

86. Another very important duty of the administrators is the avoidance of conflict of interest situations. Article 156 of the BCA states that no administrator may take part in the deliberative process of any organ of the company when having personal interests that conflict with those of the company with respect to the matter discussed. Any deliberation taken in contravention of this rule may be deemed void, and the administrator may be condemned to transfer to the company the economic benefit he obtained from it.

f. Duty to avoid insider trading

87. Very important duties are imposed specifically upon the administrators of publicly held corporations. Those, in terms of Article 155, first, second, third, and fourth paragraphs of the BCA, should refrain from privately disclosing any information not yet made public to the market that may potentially influence the value of the securities issued by the corporation. They are also prohibited from obtaining, or causing others to obtain, any advantage from privileged information and should take due care that no leakage is caused by subordinates or third parties. This rule seeks to avoid insider trading practices, which may cause damage to innocent third parties buying or selling securities, the value of which may be affected. This rule is completed by CVM Resolution No. 44, dated 23 August 2021, and Resolution No. 62, dated 19 January 2022, under which terms the administrators of publicly held corporations (as well as any other market participants) must refrain from dealing in an unfair way in Brazilian capital markets.

g. Duty to disclose shareholding

88. A last duty of administrators is their obligation to disclose any holdings of securities they retain issued by the corporation or by other companies in the same group upon being invested in their positions (Article 157 of the BCA).

V. Board of Auditors

A. General Considerations

89. Another body of the corporation to be considered is the Board of Auditors, treated in Articles 161–165-A of the BCA. It is composed of three to five Brazilian residents, independent from the corporation, that either hold university degrees or have previously served as members of the Board of Directors or the Board of Auditors of other companies for at least three years.

B. Attributes

90. The Board of Auditors may be permanent or be summoned upon the initiative of members of the corporation representing 10% of the voting capital or 5% of the non-voting capital (Article 161, second paragraph of the BCA). At any rate, it is important to stress that it is not an administrative body of the company, although its members are statutorily declared to be under the same fiduciary duties applicable to administrators. It is invested in surveillance functions, relating especially to administrators' compliance with their duties.

The Board of Auditors must also be heard by the shareholders or by the administrators, in case it is permanent or is summoned as explained above, prior to the adoption of decisions relevant to the general body of shareholders or to the corporation itself. Such relevant decisions are changes in the value of the capital, issuance of debentures or subscription bonds, investment plans, distribution of dividends, mergers, spin-offs and acquisitions involving the company. The opinions issued by the Board of Auditors are not binding as a general rule upon any organs of the corporation. They will, however, have an exceptional binding effect in case of disapproval of accounts presented by the administrators, which cannot be subsequently approved by the general meeting of shareholders.

In case the administrators or the controlling shareholders decide to act in a way contrary to the opinion of the Board of Auditors, they may incur liability based on a breach of fiduciary duty in case the Board's opinion proves to be sound.

Much criticism has been aimed at the Board of Auditors, based on the allegation that it lacks independence, since the majority of its members are nominated by the controlling shareholders. In our opinion, even if such criticism is to be partially accepted, it must be acknowledged that the action of the Board of Auditors is not altogether deprived of effectiveness. In fact, minority shareholders representing 10% of the voting capital are entitled to separately elect one of the members of the organ. The holders of non-voting preferred shares or preferred shares with restricted voting power have the same right (Article 161, fourth paragraph, item 'a' of the BCA).

As seen above, in companies in which the Board is not permanent, it can be summoned by the minority upon the occurrence of suspected irregularities. Thus, the Board of Auditors can always be summoned by the minority, and the discussion therein may be used to exert pressure on an oppressive majority.

C. *External Auditing*

91. Finally, corporations may also employ external auditors to approve their accounts, which must not be confounded with the members of the Board above. Such auditors are not organs of the company and must necessarily review the financial statements of publicly held corporations (Article 177, third paragraph of the BCA).

§4. Liquidation of the Corporation

I. Introduction

92. Liquidation is the procedure according to which the remaining creditors of a wound up corporation are paid prior to distribution to former shareholders of their respective participation in the corporation's remaining assets. Only after the liquidation will the legal personality of a corporation be extinguished (Articles 207 and 219, item I, of the BCA).

The liquidation procedure to be adopted basically depends on the reasons that cause the company to wind up, that is, the reason why the associative relationship between the shareholders is terminated. Accordingly, there are three different forms of winding up for a corporation, as foreseen in the BCA. Those forms could be indicated as voluntary or automatic winding up, winding up by the court and special winding up, as seen below.

II. Voluntary or Automatic Winding Up

93. Article 206 of the BCA establishes that the corporation will be automatically wound up:

- when its term of duration, as set forth in the by-laws, has expired (it is possible that such a term is indicated in the by-laws as 'indefinite');
- in the other cases established in the by-laws;

- when the general shareholders' meeting decides in this sense or verifies that the corporation has been left with only one shareholder, if the minimum number of two shareholders is not re-established until the succeeding ordinary shareholders' meeting (*see* paragraph 28 above); and
- by reason of extinction of the governmental authorization in the case of a corporation depending on such an authorization in view of its field of activity.

In these cases, the by-laws may preordain the winding up procedures and establish rules as to the appointment of the liquidator and the persons to take office on the Board of Auditors during the liquidation. If the by-laws do not establish such procedures, the general meeting of shareholders is to do so (Article 208 of the BCA).

In case the corporation has a Board of Directors, the general meeting may resolve that its members shall be kept in office during the liquidation, and in this case, it will be the Board's duty to appoint the liquidator. The body that has appointed the liquidator (the general meeting of either the shareholders or the Board of Directors) may dismiss him at any time.

III. Judicial Liquidation

94. A corporation may also be dissolved by order of the court. That will occur (Article 206, item II):

- in case a shareholder obtains judicial cancellation of the incorporation, that is, when the courts verify that a relevant legal requirement was not met at the time of the corporation's formation;
- in case that, by means of a judicial procedure initiated by shareholders representing 5% or more of the corporate capital, it is proved that the corporation is not capable of fulfilling its corporate objects; or
- in case of the corporation's bankruptcy, as per the specific legislation.

In these cases, the liquidator will be appointed by the court instead of by the shareholders' general meeting or the Board of Directors, as in the previous cases (Article 209, sole paragraph, of the BCA).

A winding up determined by the court will also take place when the administrative bodies or the controlling shareholders frustrate the voluntary or automatic winding up of a company, as described above (Article 209, item I, of the BCA).

Additionally, in case of extinction of the governmental authorization, when such an authorization is necessary, winding up by the court may be requested by a public prosecutor if the corporation does not initiate the applicable winding up procedures within thirty days or in case it interrupts such procedures for more than fifteen days (Article 209, item II, of the BCA).

IV. Special Winding Up

95. A corporation may be subject to a special winding up procedure whenever its activities are specifically governed by special regulations and supervised by a governmental authority, which will also decide on its winding up. In those situations, the corporation's winding up is to follow the procedures indicated in the applicable special legislation.

One example of such legislation is Law No. 6024, dated 13 March 1974, which regulates the administrative liquidation of financial institutions and other similar entities (brokerage houses and the like).

Such liquidations will occur by order of the Central Bank of Brazil, which has the authority to supervise and regulate financial activities. The Central Bank will decree a financial institution's winding up basically when it fails to meet its duties before its creditors, when the actions of its managers tend to risk the creditors' rights or fail to comply with the applicable banking regulations, or when the company is not liquidated within ninety days from the cancellation by the Central Bank of Brazil of its authorization to do business in the financial markets. In these cases, the Central Bank of Brazil appoints the liquidator and supervises the liquidation procedures.

V. The Liquidator

96. The liquidator is the person charged with the legal representation of the corporation being wound up, having authority to sell its assets, if necessary, in order to complete the liquidation (Article 211 of the BCA).

The liquidator must be authorized by the general shareholders' meeting if any burden is to be imposed on the corporation's assets or a loan is to be received on its behalf (unless urgent payments are to be made) (Article 211, sole paragraph, of the BCA). The liquidator has the same liabilities applicable to administrators of a company (Article 217 of the BCA).

Besides taking over all of the executive functions in the corporation, the liquidator will collect its assets, conclude ongoing businesses, receive credits, pay debts, distribute the remaining assets among the shareholders, and convene shareholders' meetings when necessary or convenient (Article 210 of the BCA).

It is worth mentioning that, during the winding up procedure, the restrictions on the voting rights eventually imposed on preferred shares (*see* paragraph 39) will be suspended, and consequently, all shares will bear equal voting rights (Article 213, first paragraph of the BCA).

While paying the debts of the corporation, the liquidator must observe the rights of preferred creditors. Further, he shall pay the debts proportionally to the funds available, without distinctions between debts already due and falling due in the future, although he shall apply discounts when paying the latter, if they are subject to pro rata bank interest rates (Article 214 of the BCA).

After the debts have been paid and the remaining assets distributed to the shareholders, the liquidator will submit a final report for the approval of the general meeting of shareholders. Dissenting shareholders as to that approval must initiate any applicable legal procedure that they deem convenient within thirty days from the corresponding general meeting (Article 216 of the BCA).

Once the liquidation of a corporation is concluded, its shareholders may be sued by a creditor only up to the amounts returned to them. However, it will always be possible for such a creditor to sue the liquidator for damages, if applicable (Article 218 of the BCA).

§5. Mergers, Consolidations, and Spin-Offs

I. General Characteristics and Meaning

97. Mergers, consolidations, and spin-offs are operations leading to the concentration of business enterprises. This has been a marked trend in modern economics, which legislatures have partly tried to forestall through the issuance of anti-trust legislation.

The meaning assigned to the word merger in common-law practice is wide enough to embody two legal forms permitted in Brazilian legislation. The first of those is the merger in which one of two companies absorbs the assets of the other, which is extinguished. This is called '*incorporação*' in Brazilian law (Article 227 of the BCA). However, a merger may occur where two or more companies consolidate in one new legal entity, what is called '*fusão*' in Brazilian law (Article 228 of the BCA), and to which we may refer here as consolidation. Both forms of merger are given a rather detailed statutory treatment in the BCA, bearing many procedural similarities to the mechanism adopted in the US.

Besides '*fusão*' and '*incorporação*', Brazilian law also admits that the assets of a company be split and attributed to other legal entities already in existence or specially created for the purpose, with or without disappearance of the original company. This is called *cisão* in Brazilian law (Article 229 of the BCA), being also considered a form of economic concentration, to which we may refer here as a spin-off. That is because the division of assets occurring in the spin-off is normally incidental to a company reorganization in which part of the original enterprise is to be sold or transferred to other economic groups. Brazilian law has opted to regulate the spin-off as a separate legal formulation. It is subject to certain formalities that entail both the transfer of the assets and the winding up of the original corporation, if necessary. This is different from both American and English law, in which a spin-off is to be effected in approach through a transfer of assets, followed by extinction of the transferring entity.

II. Legal Nature of Mergers, Consolidations, and Spin-Offs

98. It is an interesting exercise to inquire into the legal nature of mergers, consolidations, and spin-offs. They are normally seen as issuing from a contract between the legal entities involved. This view has, however, been criticized on the grounds that the key feature in the transactions analysed herein is the transfer of a business entity's assets as a whole.[17]

III. Procedural Steps and Documentation in Mergers, Consolidations, or Spin-Offs

99. The contractual theory is grounded on the fact that mergers, consolidations, and spin-offs in Brazilian law are initiated by a protocol to be executed by the administrators or members of the legal entities involved, which is considered to bear a contractual nature. The legal entities whose administrators or members should execute said instrument are both the surviving and the disappearing legal entity in case of '*incorporação*', both consolidating entities in the case of '*fusão*' and the entity transferring assets and any entity already in existence in the case of a split up (Article 224 of the BCA). If, conversely, the assets are transferred in a spin-off to an entity to be created in the process of a spin-off, the latter and its members and administrators must not execute the protocol, and because of that, no contract can be envisaged in this hypothesis.

The protocol, in terms of Article 224 of the BCA, must indicate the basic conditions to which the merger, spin-off or consolidation is subject, which include the precise definition of the criteria for evaluating the net worth of the entities involved. Such evaluation may be made according to the book value of the net worth, monetarily indexed, in the absence of specific legal rules on the subject. The employment of market value – or other criteria established by the CVM in case of publicly held corporations – is only required in case of a merger involving a subsidiary and its parent company (please refer to the concept of subsidiary described in paragraph 107 below), in terms of Article 264, second and fourth paragraphs of the BCA. When applicable, the protocol should also fix the rate according to which the substitution of shares in any company extinguished (or whose assets are partially transferred to others) in any new entity or company created by the merger, consolidation, and spin-off is to be made. The class and characteristics of the new shares should also be described, together with the value of any increase in the capital of entities receiving assets in the transactions described herein. These provisions take account of the fact that mergers, spin-offs and consolidations are operations that indirectly affect the shareholders of entities transferring assets to others, who are to be compensated for such transference through the receipt of shares in the entities benefited by the transfer, such shares to correspond in value to the benefit obtained.

The protocol is primarily an agreement entered into by members or administrators of the entities involved in the operations of merger, spin-off and consolidation. It is thus deemed to be a pre-contract by Brazilian legal doctrine, in the sense that it must be followed by other acts implementing the operations. Such implementation is the approval of the protocol by the general meeting of shareholders or similar bodies of

17. Mauro Brandão Lopes, *A Cisão no Direito Societário Brasileiro* (São Paulo: Revista dos Tribunais, 1980), 98 ff.

the companies or entities whose members and/or administrators have signed the protocol. Through this act, they express their consent to the contents of the said document, adhering to its terms.

The protocol is not really a pre-contract, in our opinion, since it does not embody an obligation of the parties to enter into another contract in the future. In fact, it is the only valid contract grounding the operations described herein, being executed first by the administrators, shareholders, and/or members of the entities involved and subsequently by the entities themselves through ratification by their deliberative organs. The protocol, in terms of Article 225 of the BCA, will be submitted for the approval of the general meeting of shareholders or similar bodies of the entities involved, accompanied by a letter of justification. Such letter shall contain an explanation of the reasons underlying the merger, consolidation, or spin-off.

The meeting of shareholders approving the operation shall designate experts for evaluating the assets transferred in the operations of merger, spin-off and consolidation (Articles 227, first paragraph, 228, first paragraph, and 229, second and third paragraphs of the BCA). No requirements are normally imposed as to the qualification of such experts, except in the case of a merger involving a subsidiary and its parent company. In this case, the law deems the risk of undervaluation of assets of the company disappearing in the merger to be high, so as to impair the rights of the minority through the reduction of their entitlement to shares. As a protection, Article 264 and its paragraphs of the BCA require that three experts or a specialized firm prepare the report. As already stressed above, for the same reasons, their evaluation must be based on market value – or other criteria established by the CVM in case of publicly held corporations – when a subsidiary and its parent company are involved. The evaluator's report will subsequently need to be approved by a general meeting of shareholders or similar bodies of the company or entity receiving the assets in case of a merger, spin-off or consolidation in which the assets are transferred to an already existing entity. In any spin-off in which the assets are transferred to a new company or entity, the report of the experts does not have to be approved after it is presented, since they will not mix with any other assets existing in the new company not originating from the original company or entity. In case of a consolidation, in which the assets of both entities involved are bound to mingle in only one company or entity, it will be necessary to obtain the approval of the members or partners of both companies or entities, united in one single meeting, regarding the report presented by the experts. In this meeting, members or partners of one company or entity will be prevented from voting on the reports on the assets of the company or entity they integrate (Article 228, second paragraph of the BCA). The approval described in this paragraph will be a condition for the entering into force of the terms of the operations.

On 1 September 2008, the CVM approved Orientation Opinion No. 35, which reinforced the administrators' duties on mergers, consolidations and spin-offs involving publicly held corporations and their controlling shareholders, controlled companies or companies under common control. Under such Orientation Opinion, the administrators of publicly held corporations shall create mechanisms that ensure to the shareholders that their fiduciary duties in connection with the negotiation of the relevant corporate restructure were duly observed. Among other mechanisms, Orientation Opinion No. 35 suggests the formation of an independent committee responsible for negotiating the terms of the merger, consolidation or split-offs. Although the Orientation Opinion No. 35 is not binding on publicly held corporations, such committee has been formed in the context of large corporate restructures performed since its enactment.

IV. The Principle of Protection of the Value of Shares in Mergers, Consolidations, and Spin-Offs

100. The capital of the company or entity receiving the assets transferred may not at any rate be increased by a value higher than the value attributed to the assets transferred (Article 226 of the BCA). It is an arguable point in view of such a rule whether companies or entities presenting a negative net worth can disappear in a merger, consolidation, or spin-offs, being consolidated in another company or entity to be created. The best conclusion is based on the fact that Article 226 of the BCA does not require the capital of the company receiving the assets to be increased in absolute terms, and thus, a merger in these conditions would be lawful. Such a merger may, however, be objectionable by the minority on the basis that it is an abuse of power by the majority of a profitable company to induce the absorption of a negative net worth (Article 117 of the BCA).

Obviously, such allegation will be refutable in case the company or entity bearing a negative net worth presents hidden reserves (e.g., goodwill, non-recognized appreciation in value of fixed assets) in an amount sufficient to make good the loss.

A related problem is the discussion of the possibility of a company receiving a given proportion of the assets of a company or entity undergoing a spin-off being attributed liabilities in a proportion higher or lower than that which the assets received bear to the total net worth of the transferor company. This is accepted in the French system, being a debated and not definitively resolved matter in Brazil. According to Article 229 of the BCA, a spin-off involves the transfer of part of the patrimony of a company. The concept of patrimony embodies both assets and liabilities, and thus, a part of it must contain assets and liabilities bearing an identical proportion to the whole.

In view of that, it is our opinion that no spin-off according to irregular proportions of assets and liabilities would be theoretically feasible. It must, however, be conceded that such spin-off can be found rather frequently in Brazilian business practice.[18]

V. Protection of Third Parties

101. It is obvious that the transactions described herein, as long as they have the transfer of assets as their main feature, may substantially affect the rights of members or creditors of the companies involved. In view of that, many statutory rules have been introduced to protect such interests.

---

18. Karl Larenz, *Derecho Civil – Parte General*, Madrid, 17th para. 404 ff.

A. Protection of Shareholders

102. As to the shareholders, it is first to be stressed that their interests will be damaged whenever the assets of a company are transferred at a lower value or received by a value above market value in mergers or spin-offs. The decision as to the operations described above is to be taken by the majority, and the solution found by the BCA (Articles 136, 137, and 230) is to create the right of withdrawing from the corporation in favour of minority shareholders. At this point, it is important to remark that the legal protection introduced by the law has a flaw, since it extends exclusively to shareholders or partners of a company disappearing in a merger, as well as to those shareholders of a company transferring assets in a spin-off. This leaves the shareholders of the absorbing company or partnerships in a merger without protection, as well as those receiving assets in a spin-off. They also deserve protection since they incur the risk that the assets of the company undergoing consolidation or spin-off will be received at a value above their market value. This risk is unaccounted for in legislation, with the result being that the minority is left only with the protection afforded by the rules on liability of controlling shareholders for oppression of the minority contained in Article 117 of the BCA (paragraph 72 above).

In pursuance of the right of withdrawing described above, the corporation will be obliged to acquire the holding of minority shareholders by the value established in the by-laws, which may only be less than the net worth of the shares stated in the last balance sheet approved by the shareholders' general meeting, if the refund value is calculated in accordance with the economic value of the corporation (Article 45, first paragraph, of the BCA).

In relation to mergers and consolidations, the right to refund shall be restricted to shares that have neither liquidity nor dispersion in the market (Article 137, II of the BCA). Liquidity exists whenever the shares are included in a stock exchange index in Brazil or abroad, and dispersion occurs when the same individual or legal entity does not hold directly or indirectly one-half of the shares of the same type and class. In relation to spin-off, the right to refund shall only exist in case the operation entails a change in the corporate objects (except when the assets are directed to a company the prevailing object of which is equal to that of the spin-off entity), reduction in the minimum dividend or participation in a group of companies (Article 137, III of the BCA).

An exception to such general rules is introduced in case of a merger involving a subsidiary and its parent company. In this hypothesis, the rights of the minority have been found to deserve special protection. In terms of Article 264, second and third paragraphs, of the BCA, the shares held by the controlling company in the subsidiary will be evaluated at their net worth. Such value will be calculated based on the market value of the assets of the company in which the shares are held or according to other criteria approved by the CVM, in the case of publicly held corporations. The value of the shares thus calculated should be employed as a parameter for calculating the quantity of shares to be attributed to the minority shareholders of the company being extinguished, whose market value has been determined in the way described above. This is not a legal obligation but just a condition which, if not complied with, will vest minority shareholders of the company disappearing in the merger with the right to retire against indemnification calculated through special rules. In case this condition is verified, the shareholders dissenting from the resolution of the general meeting of the controlled corporation that approved the transaction may opt to be refunded based on the net worth value of their shares, as described in the first part of this paragraph. Such right will not exist in case the shares meet cumulatively the requirements of liquidity and dispersion, as these terms are defined by Article 137, II of the BCA, in which case the law considers that the shareholder can obtain adequate protection by selling the shares in the market.

As a last observation on the topic, it must be pointed out that the criticism made above on the lack of protection of shareholders or members of the companies not disappearing in the merger is also applicable to transactions involving a parent company and its subsidiary.

B. Protection of Creditors

103. The interest of creditors is also the aim of special rules towards their protection. This is because a company's assets constitute the basic guarantee of its creditors, and such assets are transferred to new companies in mergers, consolidations, and spin-offs.

An extensive protection is granted to debenture holders, who must grant their prior approval to any operation implying a merger, consolidation, or spin-off of the corporation issuing debentures (Article 231 of the BCA). Such approval will, however, be unnecessary in case the corporation enables the debenture holders to redeem the value of the securities at any time within six months from the date the minutes of the general meeting of shareholders that approve the merger, consolidation, or spin-offs are published. It must be remarked that this provision is not a complete protection for debenture holders, since it does not extend to holders of securities issued by the company absorbing assets in incorporation or spin-off, whereas the net worth of the company of which the assets are being absorbed may be negative as seen above.

Such gaps in the legal protection of debenture holders are, however, filled by the statutory protection conferred upon creditors in general, a category in which the former are included. Such protection is broader since it extends to creditors of any of the companies taking part in mergers or spin-offs. In terms of Article 232 of the BCA, the creditors of any company involved in a merger may object to the operation within sixty days from the date the acts relating to the operation are published, such publication being a requirement for efficacy of the operation before third parties. In case the company is wound up in the sixty-day term mentioned above, the creditors may ask for the splitting of the assets of the company issuing from the merger or consolidation in such a way as to restore the situation preceding the merger. At any rate, the companies involved in the merger or consolidation may prevent the exercise of the creditors' right of opposition by judicially depositing the value due to the complaining creditor or providing for a surety, in case such a value is then ascertainable.

As for the spin-off, as a general rule, the companies to which assets are transferred shall succeed the transferring company in the liabilities assigned in the documents pertaining to the transaction. However, this is extended by Article 233 of the BCA, under which terms companies receiving assets in a spin-off and those transferring assets (if they continue to exist) will be jointly and severally liable for debts prior to the spin-off. In a spin-off in which the company or entity transferring assets does not disappear, it is possible to exclude joint and several liability by express provision in the protocol. In such case, however, any creditor of the company undergoing a spin-off may prevent the exclusion from applying to its credit by notifying the company within ninety days counted from the date the documents relating to the operation are published, such publication being a requirement for the efficacy of the operation before third parties, as seen above.

VI. Mergers, Consolidations, and Spin-Offs of Other Types of Business Associations

104. Until the enactment of the new BCC in 2002, the rules mentioned in this chapter on mergers, consolidations, and spin-offs were extended to any form of business association, whether corporations or partnerships. However, the BCC addresses mergers, consolidations, and spin-offs of partnerships and limited liability companies from Articles 1116–1122, establishing general rules very similar to the ones already adopted for corporations.

§6. Groups of Companies, Holding Companies, and Subsidiaries

I. Basic Forms of Concerns

105. The previous section dealt with proceedings tending to unify several legal entities for the conducting of business. However, Brazilian legal regulation of corporations also permits structures according to which one business enterprise is conducted under a unified direction but divided among several legal entities. The same structures may be used for conducting separate activities constituting more than one business enterprise by the diversity of their scope. These latter structures will be examined in this section.

In a first approach, it must be said that three such structures exist. The first is the formation of a parent-subsidiary relationship, in which a degree of subordination is introduced into the relationship between two or more companies, without being expressly declared for external purposes as an economic unity. The second structure is the group of companies formally constituted and expressly declared for external purposes as an economic unity, in which some legal entities are subordinated to others. Finally, the third structure, the so-called *consórcio*, is formally declared as a business and economic unity before third parties, but it does not imply any form of subordination among the companies composing it.

II. Relationship among Companies

106. Turning to the first of the above-mentioned structures, it must be said that a holding company and its subsidiaries or associated companies are undeniably an economic, and frequently also an entrepreneurial, unity. They are treated as such by the legislation, which seeks to define the relationship among the associated companies and their relation to third parties.

A. Controlled Companies and Associated Companies

107. For legal purposes, the definition of controlled companies and associated companies is given by Article 243 of the BCA. A corporation is considered a controlled company when a controlling company has rights of a partner, either directly or through other controlled companies, which permanently assure its prevalence in voting and the power to elect the majority of the administrators. This definition is identical to that of a controlling shareholder contained in Article 116 of the BCA as a means of qualifying a controlling shareholder for liability purposes. An important difference between both definitions lies, however, in the fact that Article 243 of the BCA does not require the actual exercise of the control of the company, whereas Article 116 introduces this element as a requirement for qualification. The former provision is undoubtedly the best, given the problems already mentioned as to the meaning and interpretation raised by Article 116 of the BCA (paragraph 73 above).

According to the first paragraph of Article 243 of the BCA, corporations are associated when one of them has significant influence over the other. Pursuant to the fourth paragraph of such Article, significant influence is deemed to exist when the investing company has or exercises power to participate in the decisions referring to the financial or operational policies of the invested company without controlling it. Furthermore, a significant influence is presumed when the investing company holds a share representing 20% or more of the votes conferred by the capital stock of the invested company without controlling it (fifth paragraph of Article 243 of the BCA).

B. Disclosure Requirements and Their Relation to the Principle of Arm's Length Dealing

108. The relationship between a corporation and its controlled companies and associated companies must be subject to special rules on disclosure when a substantial link is found to exist between them. Such rules are needed to ensure that the parties entertain an arm's length relationship. In this sense, Article 247 of the BCA requires all relevant investments in controlled or associated companies to be disclosed in the financial statements of a corporation. The information to be disclosed includes the precise description of the equity held by the investing corporation, the profits of the invested company in a given year, and the debts, credits, and general results deriving from intra-group transactions.

This provision also introduces the concept of relevant investment. An equity investment of a company is relevant whenever solely considered; it represents 10% of the net worth of the investing company, or if considered jointly with all other investments in controlled and associated companies, it represents 15% of the net worth of the investing corporation.

Another important issue related to associated and controlled companies is that the investments in: (i) associated companies in which the investing company has significant influence over the management or holds at least 20% of the voting capital, (ii) controlled companies, and (iii) other companies that belong to the same group or are under common control have to be registered in the financial statements of the investing company through the equity evaluation method.

According to such method, the investing company shall yearly register the equity investments described in this item for a value equal to a portion of the accounting value of the net worth of the invested company corresponding to the percentage of the total capital of the invested company it holds. This rule is contained in Article 248 of the BCA and aims to cause investments to be realistically reflected in the balance sheets of the investing corporation. This need is based on the assumption that a corporation and its controlled and associated companies economically form one single unit. The consequence of such fact is that the economic appreciation or depreciation of the net worth of any invested subsidiary or linked company must have a direct reflection in the profit and loss account of the investing corporation. This is obtained through the evaluation of investments through the equity method, since any positive or negative variation from year to year in the net worth value of a relevant equity will be recognized as an item to be respectively added or deducted in the calculation of the profits of the investing company (Article 248, item III, of the BCA).

A consequence of the adoption of the conception that considers a corporation and its controlled and associated companies as a sole economic unit, still in the realm of disclosure requirements, is the fact that any publicly held corporation that has more than 30% of its net worth represented by investments in controlled companies shall prepare and publish, along with its own financial statements, consolidated financial statements (Article 249 of the BCA). In such financial statements, both the assets and liabilities of the investing corporation and its controlled companies will be pooled together, with the exclusion, however, of: (i) ownership, by the companies, of each other's stock; (ii) the value of any account kept between group companies; and (iii) the portions of income, of retained earnings or of accrued losses, and of the cost of inventories or of fixed assets which correspond to unrealized profits stemming from transactions between the companies.

C. Cross-Ownership

109. Restrictions are imposed by Brazilian legislation on cross-ownership between a corporation and its controlled and associated companies. The need for such restrictions derives from basically the same reasons that recommended the introduction of limitations to the ability of a company to acquire its own shares. In fact, cross-ownership represents precisely this acquisition in economic terms, with the aid of interposed companies.

A corporation investing in itself will necessarily have a distorted share capital if the amount of the investment is allowed to surpass the amount of its accumulated profits. Because of that, Article 244 of the BCA expressly prohibits cross-ownership between a corporation and its controlled and associated companies. An exception to the prohibition is introduced in case at least one of the companies involved in a circular ownership participates in the next one involved in a chain in the conditions in which a company is allowed to acquire its own shares. Such conditions are that the amount for which the investment is acquired does not exceed the amount of accumulated profits and reserves of the investing company, except for the legal reserve.[19]

The amount payable for the shares, or part of it, ordinarily represents the capital of the invested company. This correspondence would, however, be broken if the invested company could reinvest the funds in the original investor, unless such reinvestment is limited to the amount of the invested company's accumulated profits and capital surpluses. If this limit is respected, the circular chain of deleterious ownership is deemed to be broken and is consequently allowed to go unbounded. However, this will not eliminate a second setback of cross-ownerships, the fact that they may displace the attributions of the general meeting of shareholders of a company in favour of its officers. This is due to the fact that such officers will control the assets of the company, among these, shareholdings in other companies indirectly controlling or investing in the first company. Such fact would enable them to influence the voting at the general meeting of shareholders in the company they serve, reducing the role of such meeting to a mere formality. Obviously, such risk exists exclusively between controlling and controlled companies. To prevent its effects, it is a statutory provision of Article 244, second paragraph of the BCA, that all shares in controlled companies in a circular ownership structure will be deprived of voting rights.

Even the prohibition on cross-ownerships not encompassed in the exception to it is not absolute. The ownership will be allowed to continue for a maximum term of one year. After this term, the administrators of the corporation acquiring shares in another company in a way as to form a circular ownership structure will be considered jointly and severally liable for any damage caused to a third party, including the companies themselves and their shareholders (Article 244, fifth and sixth paragraph of the BCA).

In some foreign jurisdictions, such as the UK, a company may be forbidden not only from acquiring its own shares but also from giving any financial assistance for its acquisition by third parties.

This was introduced with a view to the protection of investors, who might have their interests damaged if a company was allowed to give any assistance towards the acquisition of its own shares by third parties. The purchase by a corporation of its own shares also had to be outlawed, in the words of the English legal Scholar,

19. An obligatory reserve containing 5% of the yearly profits, and not surpassing 20% of the value of the corporate capital (Art. 193 of the BCA).

Harry Rijak.[20] Such assistance would correspond to market manipulation, and Brazilian legislation has adopted a direct approach to addressing such practices. In fact, CVM Resolution No. 62/22 has expressly prohibited and defined as an infraction the creation of artificial trading conditions in the securities market.

D. Liability and Disregard of the Legal Entity

110. Another very important aspect of the economic groups formed by a corporation and its controlled and associated companies to be discussed is the liability rules to which they are submitted.

No joint or subsidiary liability is imposed in Brazilian law on controlling shareholders by the mere exercise of control. This position is different from that prevailing in developed countries, such as the US and Germany, in which there is a trend to impose subsidiary liability in cases of extensive involvement in the administration of the dependent company.[21]

This does not mean that there have been no instances in Brazil in which a corporation has been held liable for debts of its subsidiaries. Many case law instances in Brazil have applied the doctrine of disregard of the legal entity as it was originally conceived in common-law jurisdictions. Such application has, however, been restricted to cases in which fraud of the holding company, looting of corporate assets or improper use of the dependent company's legal personality (abuse of legal rights) has been proved. In fact, as per Article 50 of the Brazilian Civil Code, the disregard doctrine is to be applied by courts only in cases marked by fraud of the holding company, improper use of the dependent company's legal personality (abuse of legal rights) or looting of corporate assets. In all such cases, direct or indirect benefit to the entity being held liable for the corporations' debts should be proved, as well as evidence that such liable entity is a shareholder of the disregarded corporation.

Most of the cases putting forth this doctrine in Brazil are concerned with unpaid debts in a company's winding up, in cases in which this company has been merely created as a device for the avoidance of unlimited liability after a situation of insolvency was already present. Occasionally, the legal entity of a corporation has been disregarded, and liability imposed on its parent is based simply on the fact of a continuous exercise of a controlling power, disregarding the legal provisions above. This, however, has happened very seldom and in cases in which a strong imbalance between the economic position of the indebted corporation and that of its creditors could be found. Thus, the legal entity of an insurance company has been disregarded to the benefit of an impoverished widow. These kinds of decisions tend to be rare and isolated and determined exclusively by equity considerations specific to the case. Thus, as a rule, it can be said that no liability will normally be imposed on a

20. *A Sourcebook of Company Law*, 872 (Jordans Bristol, 1989).

21. *See* in Germany the so-called Autokran decision in 95 BGHZ 330 (1985) and in the US the case In re Oil Spill by the 'Amoco Cadiz' off the Coast of France on 16 Mar. 1978 MDL 376 (N.D. Ill 18 Apr. 1984).

corporation based on acts of its subsidiary or linked company by simple administrative influence not amounting to fraud, improper use of the legal entity concept or looting of assets.[22]

A corporation may be held liable for losses sustained by its controlled companies in case of abuse of administrative powers causing a group company to benefit any other company within the group or external to it, as well as for any of the forms of abuse of power described in Article 117 of the BCA (*see* paragraph 73 above). Article 246 of the BCA allows minority shareholders to act in this case through the means of derivative actions. The liability will also exist in relation to damages eventually caused to associated companies by virtue of the general provisions contained in Article 186 of the BCC. According to such provisions, whoever commits wrong acts or omissions that cause damage to others should provide compensation for the loss.

These rules have, as their main purpose, the imposition of liability in case the link between the several companies in an economic group is used by the leading company in the group to obtain benefits for itself or to bestow benefits on others through transactions not at arm's length involving group companies. They are further reinforced by Article 245 of the BCA, which expressly extends the risk of liability to the administrators of any group company that is damaged by entering into transactions not at arm's length.[23]

E. *Wholly Owned Subsidiaries*

111. Brazilian law regarding entrepreneurial concerns admits as well a structure representing a middle course between the parent-subsidiary relationship between two independent legal entities and a merger, as described in paragraph 97 above. Such structure is the wholly owned subsidiary, which resembles the former in its formal characteristics and liability rule and the latter in the exclusion of shareholders external to the group.

Wholly owned subsidiaries are permitted by Article 251 of the BCA, which establishes that a company incorporated under Brazilian laws may be the sole shareholder of another corporation. This is an exception to the contractual nature attributed to Brazilian corporations and partnerships in general, in pursuance of which, normally, at least two ownerships or partners are required for the incorporation of such bodies. Their main advantage is the possibility of separation of assets for carrying on an activity under the cover of limited liability, without, however, the need to admit co-members whose interests would have to be taken into account, thus impairing the subordination of the interests of the wholly owned subsidiary to those of the parent company. This does not mean, however, that a parent company of a wholly owned subsidiary will escape any liability whatsoever. In fact, it will be

22. *See* in this sense unanimous decision, 4a Câmara Cível, Tribunal de Justiça do Estado do Rio de Janeiro, 5 Nov. 1988, RT, 631: 198.
23. *See* in this sense Embargos Infringentes No. 381. 690, Sao Paulo, dated 18 Oct. 1988.

liable for abuses of power causing damage to the interests of creditors, the employees of the company and the community in general, in terms of the above-mentioned Articles 116 and 117 of the BCA (*see* paragraph 73 above).

A wholly owned subsidiary may come into existence through three legal techniques. The first is its direct incorporation through a public deed by a Brazilian company. The second is the acquisition by such a Brazilian company of all the shares in an already existing corporation. The third form of acquisition is similar to the German institute called *Eingliederung*,[24] in which a company holding more than 95% of the stock of a subsidiary may require the compulsory transfer of the rest of the shares, forming an integrated concern. The BCA provides, in its Article 252, that a Brazilian company may submit to the general meeting of shareholders of another Brazilian company a proposal to have such a company converted into a wholly owned subsidiary of the offering company.

The shareholders of the subsidiary should receive, in exchange for the shares to be transferred by them, a corresponding equity in the transferee company to be subscribed to by the transferor company in the name of its shareholders. The operation must be approved by the general meeting of both the transferor and transferee companies involved through the same procedures and documentation required for a merger (Articles 224 and 225 of the BCA). The approval by the company to transfer its shares must be given by shareholders representing an absolute majority of the voting capital. In both companies, the approval of the integration of another company as a wholly owned subsidiary will grant dissenting shareholders a right of withdrawal against indemnification.

Under the terms of Article 253 of the BCA, the parent company of a wholly owned subsidiary may at any moment choose to sell part of the shares in the latter or to increase its capital, admitting new members. In such a case, the shareholders in the parent company will have a right of first refusal in the acquisition or subscription of the shares, in the proportion of the stake detained by them.

III. Formally Constituted Groups of Companies

A. General Characteristics and Formation

112. Another very important economic concern permitted in Brazilian law is the de jure group of companies. Such a group may be legally created through proper formalities by a corporation and its controlled companies under the terms of Article 265 of the BCA. The controlling corporation around which the group is organized must be incorporated according to Brazilian laws. There is no prohibition on its control from abroad. According to Article 269 of the BCA the de jure concern will be constituted by a so-called group agreement to be approved by all the group companies, containing the following items: (i) the designation to be given to the group; (ii) the name of the leading corporation in the group and of its subsidiaries; (iii) the conditions under which the several group companies participate in the association; (iv) the rules for admission or exclusion of other companies in or from the group;

24. Aktiengesetz, ss 319–320.

(v) the structure of the administration of the group; (vi) the requirements for alteration of the group agreement; and (vii) the nationality of the group.

At this point, it must be stressed that in terms of Article 269 of the BCA, the criteria for determining a group's nationality will be the place of residence of the individuals controlling the leading corporation in a group. This definition of nationality is, however, exclusively valid for formal purposes, that is, for the definition of the nationality of the group to be inscribed in the group agreement as per item (vii) above. This must not be understood as requiring the leading corporation in a group to be under national control as a condition for its formation, since, as noted above, Article 265 clearly states that incorporation according to Brazilian laws shall suffice.

Once prepared, the group agreement must be approved by the general meeting of shareholders of all group companies. Such approval will be subject to the same requirements applicable to amendments to the by-laws of the company, and a right of withdrawal will be granted to dissenting shareholders (Article 270 of the BCA).

After such approval, the agreement should be registered, along with the minutes of the meetings of shareholders of the several group companies approving it, in the companies' registrar with jurisdiction over the place of incorporation of the leading corporation. Additional entries should be made with registrars having jurisdiction over other group companies.

Once formed, a group should annually publish consolidated financial statements in the form prescribed in paragraph 108 above, to be presented jointly with the financial statements of the leading group company (Article 275 of the BCA).

B. Liability

113. The very feature of the de jure group of companies to be stressed is the liability rules of the group companies. Whereas a corporation may not normally subordinate its interests to those of another company in the same group, this may be expressly allowed in relation to formally constituted groups of companies. In such groups, the combination of efforts, the subordination of the interests of one group company to those of others and the division among several group companies of expenses incurred or revenue obtained by one company are expressly permitted by Article 276 of the BCA. Such subordination of interests will only be accepted in terms of the group agreement existing between the parties.

The legal treatment of de jure groups in Brazilian legislation is clearly inspired by the control agreements of German law.[25] However, it may be criticized on the footing that Brazilian legislation, while copying the possibility of subordination of interests of one company to another as presented in German law, did not adopt the several guarantees that rendered this system feasible. Such guarantees seek to balance the broad powers granted to the parent by an obligation to compensate the subsidiary for all losses sustained during the period the relationship lasts. Unfortunately, no such

25. Aktiengesetz, ss 291 ff. institutes the Beherrschungsvertrag, granting the parent a broad directing power in relation to the subsidiary, and the Gewinnabfurungsvertrag, determining the transfer of the subsidiaries' profits to the parent company.

formulation exists in Brazil, where no balancing liability is imposed on the leading company in the group or on those being favoured to the detriment of other group companies. As a rule, in the absence of any provision to the contrary, the leading company will not be liable for debts of the parent. The only exception to this will be the not-so-common instances in which case law intervenes to disregard the legal personality of a company. As already stated, however, this will be limited to cases in which fraud or artificial use of legal personality can be proven (*see* paragraph 110 above).

C. Group Administration

114. The group agreement may create bodies of management at group level (Article 272 of the BCA). Such bodies may attribute collegiate deliberative powers or executive powers to those of officers of companies, and their instructions are binding on the administrators of the group companies if taken in accordance with the attributions conferred by the group agreement (Article 273 of BCA). At any rate, such bodies may not be empowered to act as representatives of the group companies before third parties. The group has no legal personality, and thus, the representation of the companies is left to their administrators.

D. Applicability of Rules Relating to Holding Companies and Subsidiaries

115. Finally, it is to be stated that the general rules applicable to holding companies and subsidiaries as such are also applicable to formally constituted groups. Among such rules, one should mention the restrictions imposed on circular ownerships and the imposition of liability in case of any subordination of interests between group companies not envisaged in the group agreement.

IV. Consortium

116. It must be pointed out that a parent-subsidiary relationship is not the only statutory form provided to enable different companies to work under unified directions. Article 278 of the BCA provides a set of rules regulating the formation of non-equity joint ventures between companies not necessarily linked by the subordination ties of a parent-subsidiary relationship. Such structure is called a consortium and has no legal personality according to Brazilian law.

The consortium is constituted to carry out a specific activity, either of a continuing or of a transient nature. The debts incidental to carrying out such activity will be attributed to the individual company incurring it, and no joint and several liability may be imposed on other members of the consortium, unless otherwise determined in the agreement of the consortium.

The consortium is formed through an agreement to be registered with the registrar of companies with jurisdiction over the place of its siege. Such contract shall indicate the members of the consortium, its object, the obligations and rights of each member company, and rules on its administration and decision-making process, among others (Article 279 of the BCA).

§7. Taxation of Corporations and Shareholders

I. Introduction

117. In Brazil, a corporation is subject to a wide variety of taxes. Normally its profits will be subject to income taxes (Corporate Income Tax – *Imposto de Renda da Pessoa Jurídica* 'IRPJ' and *Contribuição Social sobre o Lucro Líquido* – Social Contribution on Net Profit 'CSLL') and its revenues will be subject to taxes on gross revenues (*Contribuição para o Programa de Integração Social* – Social Integration Program 'PIS' and *Contribuição para o Financiamento da Seguridade Social* – Contribution for the Financing of Social Security 'COFINS'). Moreover, a number of other charges having a social character and/or introduced in the interest of different professions, underdeveloped regions of the country, etc., are also levied. There are also several additional federal, state and municipal taxes, such as those levied on the value added to goods (merchandise) and industrialized products, import and export taxes, service taxes, taxes on the ownership of vehicles and of real estate, taxes on the transfer of the assets, and tax on credit, currency exchange, insurance, and securities transactions.

It is worth noting that such scenario may change within the next years, as the Brazilian Government has proposed, and Congress is currently discussing a significant tax reform on consumption/sales taxes. Discussions revolve around the consolidation/unification and simplification of several state, municipal, and federal taxes into two new value added taxes on goods and services – one federal and one state/municipal. There would also be a selective excise tax to discourage the consumption of certain products deemed harmful. It is likely that the transition to this new system, if approved by Congress, would take a few years. The Brazilian Government also intends to propose an income tax reform, of which the most relevant change is likely to be the reinstitution of income tax (WHT) on dividend distributions. As of November 2023, the income tax reform plan has not yet been presented by the Government. Nonetheless, several existing bill proposals currently being discussed by Congress may also affect this taxation.[26]

26. Such as WHT on dividend distributions, with an increased rate for beneficiaries located in tax havens or subject to a privileged tax regime (Bill 2,337/2021); reduction of the Corporate Income Tax (IRPJ) rate (*see* https://g1.globo.com/economia/noticia/2023/08/11/governo-vai-propor-reducao-do-ir-de-pessoa-juridica-na-proxima-etapa-da-reforma-tributaria-diz-secretario.ghtml); non-deductibility of Interest on Net Equity (INE) (Bill 4,258/2023); taxation of capital gains earned on indirect transfers out of Brazil of assets located in Brazil (Bill 2,337/2021).

II. Income Tax

118. According to Article 43 of the Brazilian National Tax Code (Law No. 5172, dated 25 October 1966), income tax shall be levied on income of any nature.

Corporate income tax ('IRPJ') applies at a 15% rate plus an additional surtax of 10% for annual taxable income exceeding BRL 240,000.00 or quarterly taxable income exceeding BRL 60,000.00. The tax treatment of capital gains is usually similar to that applicable to ordinary income; capital gains must be included within the taxable profits for purposes of corporate taxation.

There are basically two tax regimes available for calculating corporate income tax: (i) the real or actual profit regime (*lucro real*), and (ii) the presumed profit regime (*lucro presumido*). Legal entities must elect one of these regimes at the beginning of the calendar year and shall abide by the elected method during the whole calendar year. It is generally not possible to change the regime during the calendar year. Some legal entities are legally obliged to the real profit regime, as detailed below.

Under the real/actual profit regime, corporate income tax may be calculated on a quarterly or annual basis upon the company's net accounting profits adjusted by additions and deductions provided by the Income Tax legislation (this adjusted taxable profit is denominated 'real' or 'actual' profit). Companies that elect the annual basis calculation (more common) must make advance monthly payments of IRPJ calculated either on an estimated basis (equivalent to a percentage of gross revenues from core business activities, as defined by the Brazilian tax legislation, plus 100% of any other income/revenues/gains) or upon the real profit, whichever is lower. At the end of each calendar year, the company must appraise the real annual profit on 31 December and either collect any additional IRPJ due, request a refund or offset any IRPJ overpaid during the year.

Tax loss carry-forwards from previous tax periods ('NOLs') can be used by companies to offset taxable profits in any given fiscal year up to the limit of 30% of the taxable profits in the real profit regime. Non-operational NOLs can usually only be offset in subsequent tax periods against profits of the same nature. There is no statute of limitations for the use of NOLs. There may be, however, certain restrictions to the use of NOLs in corporate reorganizations or where the company goes through a change of control and business activity. For companies taxed under the real profit regime, thin capitalization rules set forth certain limits for the tax deductibility of debt interest owed by Brazilian companies to related parties overseas or to persons located in tax haven jurisdictions (as defined by Brazilian laws). Such limits are determined with reference to the level of indebtedness of the Brazilian entity vis-à-vis its net equity. Tax deductibility of payments to tax havens, in general, is subject to specific legal requirements.

Under the presumed profit regime, corporate income tax must be paid on a quarterly basis and is calculated at the same rates (15%, plus 10% surtax for presumed profits exceeding BRL 60,000.00 per quarter) over a presumed basis, which corresponds to a percentage of the company's gross revenues from core business activities (as defined by the Brazilian tax legislation) plus 100% of any other income/revenues/gains. The percentages to calculate the presumed basis depend on the company's line of business. For activities such as the sale of goods, the presumed basis corresponds to 8% of gross revenues, while 32% applies to most service companies. This regime does not allow deductions of expenses, costs, and losses from the tax basis nor offsetting of NOLs. Companies must comply with certain legal requirements in order to elect the presumed profit method, of which the most relevant are: (i) total revenues in the previous calendar year must not exceed the current limit of BRL 78,000,000 (an amount to be reduced proportionally in case the months of a given tax period are less than twelve); and (ii) the company cannot earn profits, capital gains or income from overseas (with certain exceptions for export revenues). Certain companies, such as financial institutions and assimilated entities, factoring companies, and those that explore credit securitization activities or that benefit from tax exemptions or reductions, are not eligible for the presumed taxation system.

Transactions of Brazilian entities with related parties overseas or with persons located in tax havens (as defined by Brazilian laws) are subject to Brazilian Transfer Pricing (TP) rules. The Brazilian TP system was completely overhauled in 2023 in order to meet OECD's TP standards. Starting in January 2024, the Brazilian TP system will be fully aligned to the Arm's Length Principle and to the TP methods recognized by the OECD.

Dividends paid by Brazilian companies to any local or foreign resident shareholders (individuals or legal entities) are currently exempt from Brazilian Income Tax with respect to profits appraised after 1 January 1996.

Brazilian companies that have current or retained profits are allowed to pay or credit Interest on Net Equity (INE) to their stakeholders. As opposed to regular dividend distributions, INE is generally subject to a 15% Withholding Income Tax (WHT), but amounts paid or credited as INE are deductible for corporate income tax purposes for companies in the real profit regime, subject to certain legal limits. For this reason, distributing INE may be more tax-efficient than distributing regular dividends. Said WHT is an advance payment of the corporate income tax due if the beneficiary is a legal entity domiciled in Brazil or definitive taxation if the beneficiary is a Brazilian resident individual or a non-Brazilian resident. WHT generally applies at the mentioned 15% rate on INE paid to persons resident or domiciled abroad, but such rate is 25% if the beneficiary is located in a tax haven jurisdiction (as defined by Brazilian laws).

As stated above, the Brazilian Government intends to propose an income tax reform which, among other changes, may reinstitute income tax (WHT) on dividend distributions and/or revoke the possibility of deducting INE distributions for tax purposes.

III. Withholding Income Tax (WHT)

A. *Taxation of Profits, Income, and Capital Gains of Partners Abroad*

119. As a general rule, income paid or credited to non-residents deriving from Brazilian sources or from dispositions of Brazilian assets are subject to Brazilian WHT, which is levied on an exclusive/definitive basis. The general rate is 15%, but a 25% rate is applied for ordinary service income and work remuneration, as well as for payments in general made to beneficiaries located in tax haven jurisdictions (as defined by Brazilian laws). There are a few exceptions in which the WHT rate is reduced to 0% or in which other tax rates apply, as per specific legislation. Different rates may also be provided by an applicable tax treaty between Brazil and the country where the beneficiary is resident or domiciled.

Capital gains earned by non-Brazilian residents from the sale or disposition of Brazilian assets or rights, including shares in corporate entities, are usually subject to income tax on a definitive basis at general rates that progressively range from 15% to 22.5%, according to the value of the gain. The rate is 25% if the beneficiary is located in a tax haven jurisdiction (as defined by Brazilian laws). This taxation applies even if the transaction is entered into between two non-Brazilian residents out of Brazil when the capital gain derives from a transfer/disposition of assets or rights located in Brazil, such as shares in a Brazilian corporate entity.

As previously mentioned, profits in general and dividends paid by Brazilian companies to foreign resident shareholders (individuals or legal entities) are currently exempt from Brazilian Income Tax with respect to profits appraised after 1 January 1996. Payment of INE to shareholders resident or domiciled out of Brazil is subject to WHT at a rate of 15%, except if the beneficiary is located in a tax haven jurisdiction (as defined by Brazilian laws), in which case the rate is 25%.

IV. Social Contributions

120. Certain social contributions are also levied on the operation of legal entities established in Brazil. Such are the so-called PIS, COFINS, and CSLL, the main provisions of which are described below.

A. PIS and COFINS

121. Brazilian companies are generally subject to PIS and COFINS on their gross revenues, with certain exceptions provided by the law, such as revenues from the sale or disposition of non-current assets, among others. There are currently two systems to calculate PIS and COFINS: the cumulative system and the non-cumulative system.

Most companies subject to PIS and COFINS under the non-cumulative taxation system pay such contributions at a combined rate of 9.25% (1.65% for PIS and 7.6% for COFINS) on their total revenues. The purpose of this system is to avoid the cumulative effect of these taxes in the commercial chain by granting certain tax credits, which can be used by the taxpayer to reduce PIS and COFINS payable on revenues generated by its transactions. Relevant transactions that generate PIS/COFINS credits generally include, among others: acquisition of goods for resale and acquisition of goods and services considered as raw materials or inputs for the company's manufacturing process or service provisions.

PIS and COFINS currently apply at a combined rate of 4.65% (0.65% for PIS and 4% for COFINS) on most financial revenues of legal entities subject to the non-cumulative taxation system, except for INE revenues (subject to the regular combined rate of 9.25%), and for certain foreign currency exchange and hedge revenues, which in specific situations benefit from a 0% rate.

Certain companies or types of revenues are, however, subject to PIS and COFINS calculation under the cumulative system, such as companies that calculate their corporate income taxes under the presumed profit regime, financial institutions, and companies that are subject to special tax treatment on account of their business activities. These companies pay PIS and COFINS without entitlement to any tax credits, usually at a combined rate of 3.65% (0.65% for PIS and 3% for COFINS) on their gross revenues from the sale of goods, rendering of services, transactions entered into on account or on behalf of third parties, and other revenues from the main (core business) activity. Certain revenues are also excluded from the taxable basis, such as from the sale/disposition of non-current assets, among others.

In certain cases, PIS/COFINS of an entire commercial chain may be concentrated in only one agent (*regime monofásico*), whereby manufacturers and other companies specifically set forth by the legislation are responsible for collecting PIS/COFINS due on the entire chain.

Financial institutions, entities assimilated to financial institutions, and securitization companies pay PIS/COFINS on their gross profits (gross revenues minus fund-raising expenses and other specific deductions permitted by the law) at a total combined rate of 4.65% (4% of COFINS and 0.65% of PIS).

PIS and COFINS are not levied on exports of goods abroad, on the rendering of services to individuals or legal entities resident or domiciled abroad against payment representing an inflow of currency, or on sales to trading companies specifically for export purposes.

PIS and COFINS are also levied on imports of goods and services, due by the importer generally at a total combined rate of 11.75% for imports of goods (2.1% for PIS and 9.65% for COFINS) and 9.25% for imports of services (1.65% for PIS and 7.6% for COFINS). Companies subject to the non-cumulative taxation system may also use credits of PIS and COFINS paid on certain imports (generally of goods and services considered inputs for the company's core business activities) to reduce PIS/COFINS payable on other taxable transactions.

The substitution of PIS and COFINS, together with the IPI (*Imposto sobre Produtos Industrializados*), for a single federal value-added contribution levied on sales of goods and services (under a non-cumulative system) is likely to be approved by the Brazilian Congress. However, as of the closing of this edition, the proposal is still pending approval from the Senate.

B. Social Contribution on Net Profits (CSLL)

122. The CSLL ordinarily applies to the adjusted net accounting profits of Brazilian companies, very similarly to the Corporate Income Tax (IRPJ). Its general rate is 9%, with exceptions made for certain companies such as banks, subject to a rate of 20%, and other financial institutions and private insurance companies, which are subject to a rate of 15%.

All considerations made with regard to IRPJ also apply to the CSLL, except for the applicable rates and tax basis formation in certain cases. As with IRPJ, CSLL can also be paid through real or presumed profit regimes, as per the same rules and mechanics. The only difference is that the presumed CSLL basis under the presumed profit regime, as well as the estimated CSLL basis for the advance monthly payments under the annual real profit regime, corresponds to 12% of the company's gross revenues for activities such as the sale of goods rather than the 8% applicable to IRPJ. The CSLL rate is then applied to this presumed or estimated basis.

Chapter 2. 'Sociedades Limitadas' (Limited Liability Companies)

§1. Typical Elements

I. General Characteristics

123. Besides corporations, Brazilian law permits another form of incorporated business association joining capital under the cover of limited liability rather than submitting the entire assets of the partners to the venture to the risks of a business enterprise. These are limited liability companies, the basic legal rules of which are provided for in the BCC.

Their main characteristic is that their members have their liability strictly limited to the declared capital of the company for which they are jointly and severally liable to pay up under the terms of Article 1052 of the BCC. This obligation is effective before third parties external to the company, whereas, among the members, Article 1058 of the BCC states that the party failing to pay up capital contribution may be excluded from the limited liability company, with the cancellation or transfer to third parties of the affected equity.

The limited liability companies, notwithstanding their nature of companies grouping capitals subject to limited liability, are normally indicative of a more personal relationship among the members than would be the case with corporations. This is reflected in the fact that the sole document to be filed in the formation of a limited liability company (its articles of association – '*Contrato Social*') is formally a contract. The limited liability company is brought into existence through the registration of such a document with the Registry of Commerce of the Brazilian Federal State in which the company has its headquarters, if its legal nature is entrepreneurial (see paragraph 12). If the limited liability company, however, has a non-entrepreneurial legal nature, the articles of association must be registered before the Civil Registry of Legal Entities (*Registro Civil de Pessoas Jurídicas*), a kind of notary public office that deals with legal entities.

II. Contractual Nature and Implications in Relation to Membership

A. Exclusion of Members

124. The contract in the formation of a limited liability company has been defined by Professor Tullio Ascarelli as bearing a plurilateral nature. This means that it has as many parties to it as the members of the company, each being linked to the others by an independent relationship. Such a relationship may thus be broken without implying termination of the contract as a whole, which would be the consequence of the severance of one of the parties to a normal contract. This avails the conclusion that a member of a limited liability company in breach of the contract in its articles of association may be excluded from the company by fellow members without this entailing the winding up of the company. In fact, the breach provokes only the severance of the party to the contract that is in breach of it.[27]

B. Right of Withdrawal of Dissenting Members

125. Another consequence of the plurilateral nature of the contract in the incorporation of a limited liability company is that its terms can be altered by members representing the majority of the company's capital (Article 1071, item V and Article 1076, item II of the BCC). The dissenting members will have a withdrawal right similar to that applicable to members of a corporation (Article 1077 of the BCC). Upon its exercise, they will be entitled to receive the net worth value of their interest as indicated in the special balance sheet prepared for the purpose of calculating the refund (Article 1031 of the BCC).

The withdrawal right is also granted to members dissenting from consolidation, merger, or spin-off of the company (Article 1077 of the BCC). It must be noted that the right of withdrawal in a limited liability company is broader than its corresponding right in a corporation, since all amendments to the articles of association of the former will give rise to a right of withdrawal in favour of the dissenting members.

Additionally, under general rules, the dissenting member also has a right to withdrawal independent of cause, that can be exercised at will in case of unwillingness to continue the relationship (Articles 1029 and 1053 of BCC). In this case, again, the net worth value of their interest, as indicated in the special balance sheet prepared for the purpose of calculating the refund, shall be used (Article 1031 of the BCC).

III. Taxation

126. As for taxation, limited liability companies are basically subject to the same rules applicable to corporations and any other entrepreneurial legal entities. This said, companies incorporated as small or micro companies pursuant to Complementary Law No. 123, dated 14 December 2006, may qualify for certain tax reductions and a simplified regime. The sole difference to be considered is that premium (surplus) booked as a capital reserve and paid by shareholders above the nominal value of shares subscribed in a corporation escapes taxation altogether, whereas such premium can be treated as a taxable income for limited liability companies. This difference in treatment, by the way, is questionable and can be contested in court.

IV. Limited Liability Company with a Sole Member

127. The BCC allows limited liability companies to be formed with a sole quota holder (Article 1052, first paragraph of the BCC, as amended). The sole quota holder limited liability companies follow the same rules applicable to conventional limited liability companies.

27. *Problemas das Sociedades Anônimas*, São Paulo, Saraiva, 1969, 255 ff.

By means of a sole quota holder liability company, the individual entrepreneur may isolate assets to the implementation of a certain activity, the risks of which shall only reach that isolated portion of assets. The remaining portion of assets of the entrepreneur, as a general rule, does not incur risks for the debts arising from the activity performed.

As for taxation, sole quota holder liability companies are basically subject to the same rules applicable to limited liability companies.

Sole quota holder liability companies enable individual entrepreneurs to create a legal entity in order to individually/personally develop a particular activity without minimum capital stock, with limited liability for the company's debts and separation of their personal assets from those of the entity, while still usually enabling a less burdensome taxation as compared to that applicable if the individual entrepreneur developed the same activity as a natural person.

It is not uncommon, however, for tax authorities to attempt to disregard legal entities in order to tax their income as if earned directly by the natural persons of their shareholders, claiming that the shareholders personally develop the activity and that the legal entity was created with the sole purpose of reducing taxation (tax evasion). Most of such initiatives of the tax authorities are unlawful and can be contested in courts.

§2. Applicable Rules to Limited Liability Companies

I. Quotas and Their Nature

128. The capital of a limited liability company is divided into shares called quotas. These are different from the shares issued by a corporation since they are not considered securities. Quotas bear the nature of an ensemble of rights and obligations issued from the contract entered into among the members prior to the incorporation of the company. Their incorporeal nature reflects the structural characteristics of limited liability companies, many of which are incorporated, taking into account the personal characteristics of the partners. As a consequence, the quotas into which their capital is divided are not embodied in transferable securities, implying that in business associations in which the identity of the members is not ordinarily important, their interests may not be easily transferred. This is not intended to mean that quotas in a limited liability company are not at all transferable. In case the articles of association of the company are silent, general provisions contained in the BCC (Article 1057) would come into play. According to such provisions, transfers among members are free, while quota holders may not transfer their holdings to non-members if members representing one-quarter of the capital stock expressly oppose the transfer. This rule may, however, be abolished in case a disposition as to the free transferability of quotas, regardless of consent by co-members, is itemed in the articles of association of the limited liability company.[28]

---

28. Please refer to the decisions in RE 6.639/RJ *1221* 382; Re 47.275/DJ 7 Apr. 63; RE 47.275, decided on 9 Mar. 1964; RE 34.680, decided on 27 Jan. 1958 and RE 75.680/RTJ 65/866, all argued before the Brazilian Federal Supreme Court.

A question very similar to this one is whether the quotas retained by one member in a limited liability company can be foreclosed in case executory proceedings happen to be brought against such member. Three concurring trends can be found in relation to such question. The first and most traditional position regarding the question denies the possibility of foreclosure, based on the fact that this would violate one of two principles of the law of business associations as it affects limited liability companies: it would either indicate that the company's capital could be accessed by an outsider, in case it is to be partially wound up as a result of the foreclosure, or it would lead to the admission of a member without the approval of the others. Many of the case law instances embracing such position have been based on Article 292 of the revoked part of the Brazilian Commercial Code, in terms of which private creditors of the partners or members of business associations may only foreclose the net funds detained by a member in a company, which is not a corporation, such expression interpreted as equivalent to their credits against the company. This would exclude the quotas detained in the company itself.

However, an intermediate position has subsequently developed, according to which quotas would be foreclosed whenever they could be transferred to third parties without the consent of the existing members of the company. This conciliatory view is grounded in the equitable consideration that such quotas might at any rate be transferred without the consent of the remaining members and could thus be foreclosed and attributed to the member's creditors. Finally, the third and most recent position contends that quotas in a limited liability company can be freely foreclosed by a creditor of a member under any circumstances. This is grounded on the interpretation of the term 'net funds' contained in Article 292 of the revoked part of the Brazilian Commercial Code as referring to the net worth value of the interest of a member in a given company rather than to credits. Pursuant to such interpretation, the quotas of a member might be foreclosed by creditors to pay the member's debts up to such net worth value. The last trend in favour of the possibility of a foreclosure of quotas seems to us the most reasonable and best supported by statute. It seems that it tends to prevail over the others as time goes by. Brazilian Civil Procedure Code, enacted in 2015, reinforced such view and set detailed rules to liquidate the quotas in favour of the creditor (purchase of the quotas by other partners, liquidation of the quotas with assets of the issuing company or public bidding to sell the foreclosed quotas).

II. Management Bodies

129. The BCC requires at least two management bodies: a body composed of all the quota holders, the so-called quota holders' general meeting, and one or more managers, who may or may not be quota holders (Article 1060 of the BCC).

The quota holders' general meeting has the exclusive authority to: (i) approve the financial statements of the company; (ii) appoint and dismiss managers; (iii) fix the remuneration of officers; (iv) amend the articles of association; (v) decide on consolidations, mergers, and liquidation involving the company; (vi) appoint liquidators and approve their accounts; and (vii) file liquidation procedures (Article 1071 of the BCC). The proceedings and requirements involved in the establishment of the decision-making process in limited liability companies are regulated in detail by the BCC, with the objective of integrating minority shareholders into such companies. The BCC requires a certain quorum for the decisions regarding certain matters, imposes detailed rules for the calling of meetings, and guarantees a minimum of information and publicity, requiring the existence of corporate books and annual approval of the company's financial statements.

General meetings are to be held at least once a year, until the last day of the fourth month subsequent to the end of each fiscal year, in order to: (i) approve the financial statements of the company; and (ii) appoint managers (Article 1078 of the BCC). Nevertheless, they can also be held whenever any decision of the quota holders is required.

The other mandatory management body for limited liability companies is the manager or managers. Managers must be individuals and shall be appointed by the quota holders' general meeting. It will be incumbent upon such managing members to represent the company and the performance of executive functions necessary for its administration (Article 1060 of the BCC).

Limited liability companies may also choose to adopt a more complex administrative and deliberative structure similar to the one typical of a corporation (general meeting, Board of Directors, Officers, etc.). This can be legally done through ad hoc provisions introduced in the articles of association of the company.

III. Subsidiary Application of Corporations' Statutes

130. Limited liability companies are regulated by statutory provisions relating to simple partnerships in matters not covered by the rules contained in their specific chapter in the BCC (Article 1053). However, if specifically foreseen in the company's articles of association, the rules applicable to corporations may be, in a subsidiary manner, rendered applicable (Article 1053, sole paragraph, of the BCC). The company statute to be applied in this case is the BCA. Because of the inconveniences associated with the rules on simple partnerships (*Sociedades Simples*), in most cases, it is advisable to insert a clause of applicability of rules on corporations in the articles of association of limited liability companies to prevent the application of the above-mentioned partnership rules. According to DREI, the subsidiary application of corporate rules can be presumed if the limited liability company: (i) holds quotas issued by itself; (ii) issues preferred quotas; (iii) has a board of directors; (iv) has a board of auditors (DREI Normative Ruling No. 81, dated 10 June 2020). The solution in the preceding sentence is doubtful, since it contravenes statutory provisions in Article 1053 of BCC to the effect that the choice of corporate rules must be expressed.

The common opinion is that many legal provisions relating to corporations are extraneous to the legal regime applicable to limited liability companies, and these will not be applied to them, notwithstanding the generality of the terms in which the sole paragraph of Article 1053 of the BCC is drafted. Examples of such inadequate provisions are those relating to the issuance of corporate securities (shares, debentures, subscription bonds, etc.) and their negotiation on stock exchanges. This is because the framework applicable to limited liability companies does not provide for enough surveillance and transparency for them to be able to solicit funds on the market through the issuance of such securities.

Conversely, a typical instance of rules of the BCA also applicable to limited liability companies are the provisions as to liability and standards of conduct of controlling shareholders and administrators (Articles 116, 117, and 153–159 of the BCA, as per items 73 and 82–88 above). In fact, the standards of conduct and hypothesis of liability of controlling shareholders and administrators should be the same in corporations and limited liability companies, since, in both, the same causes and opportunities for oppression of the minority and breach of duties may arise. As for the liability of administrators, very similar considerations should also apply. In such instances, the more detailed provisions of the BCA, as well as their judicial construction, obviously constitute a useful augmentation to the terms of the BCC. Moreover, both statutes are in this respect compatible since they are pervaded by the idea that controlling members of a company and administrators should be held liable whenever they act in breach of the law or of the clauses in the documents filed during the company's incorporation (Article 158 of the BCA and Article 1080 of the BCC). In 2007, a new statute (Article 3 of Law No. 11638/2007) was adopted, submitting all limited liability companies with assets over BRL 240 million or annual gross revenue over BRL 300 million (called large limited liability companies or *Sociedades de Grande Porte)* to the requirements of the BCA concerning the bookkeeping and the preparation of balance sheets and other financial accounts. Despite the reform, due to issues over the interpretation of the new statute, there is still some discussion on whether the publication of these documents is compulsory for said companies.

Finally, the provisions contained in the BCA relating to holding companies and subsidiaries (Articles 243–250, as per paragraph 107 above) and to formally constituted groups of companies (Articles 265–279, as per paragraph 112 above) would also be applicable to limited liability companies. The latter may in fact have the position of either leading companies, holding companies, or subsidiaries in such inter-company relationships. They cannot, in our opinion, however, be wholly owned subsidiaries under the terms of Article 251 of the BCA (paragraph 111 above), since they necessarily bear a contractual nature under the terms of the BCC, with no possibility of exception, but for the relatively few hypotheses in which their subsistence with one sole member is allowed (paragraph 127 above). Limited liability companies may, in our opinion, be holding companies of such wholly owned subsidiaries.

Part II. Partnerships

§1. Introduction

131. In view of the many advantages provided by the corporation and the limited liability company, especially the limited liability of the partners, the partnership structure is actually seldom adopted as the framework for Brazilian business associations. Notwithstanding this, it is worthwhile to examine its main features in order to achieve a complete understanding of the law of business associations in Brazil.

§2. Main Features

132. The Brazilian partnership is characterized as a legal entity formed by parties who are interested in their mutual personal characteristics and attributes. Due to the aforesaid relevance of the personal attributes of the partners in a partnership, the withdrawal of any partner and the admission of a new one will always depend on an amendment to the articles of association.

§3. General Provisions

I. The Articles of Association and Their Requirements

133. The existence of a partnership may only be claimed among the partners and against third parties on the basis of a written instrument of agreement – the articles of association. The provisions of such a written agreement prevail over any kind of oral evidence. The articles of association may be either a private instrument or a public deed executed before a notary public and must contain under the terms of Article 997 of the BCC:

- the names, nationalities, marital status, occupation, and addresses of all partners, if individuals, or name, nationality, and address of the partners, if legal entities;
- the name, objectives, head office location, and duration of the partnership;
- the capital stock of the partnership, in Brazilian currency, with the possibility of inclusion of any assets that can be measured monetarily;
- the share of each partner in the capital stock and the manner in which it was paid;
- whether the partners are subsidiarily responsible for the partnership's obligations.

The articles of association must be filed with the Commercial Registry or with the Civil Registry of Legal Entities, depending on the entrepreneurial nature or not of the entity in formation, in order to be enforceable among the partners and against third parties, as well as for the partnership to gain its own legal personality. However, when the articles of association are not duly filed with the Commercial or Civil Registry, all of the partners may be jointly sued by third parties (Articles 985, 986, and 990 of the BCC).

II. Constructive Partnerships

134. If the written agreement is not presented, the existence of a partnership may be presumed in favour of third parties (but not in favour of the partners among each other or against third parties), based on any kind of legal evidence that indicates the present or previous association between the partners (Article 987 of the BCC).

III. The Designation of the Partnership

135. Partnerships conduct business under a designation protected by law that cannot be the object of a sale (Article 1164 of the BCC). The rules related to each corporate form establish specific requirements for entrepreneurial designation.

As a general rule, one can stress that partnerships with partners subject to unlimited liability shall operate under a designation containing the names of all unlimited partners, or at least one of them with the addition of the expression '*e companhia*', which means 'and company' (Article 1157 of the BCC). The person or persons whose name or names are utilized in the designation of the partnership will be responsible before third parties for all obligations of the latter and will have the right to charge the remaining partners for any liabilities accruing to them.

IV. Winding up of the Partnership

136. The general rule for the winding up of partnerships is stated in Article 1033 of the BCC, which sets forth that partnerships shall terminate upon: (i) the expiration of the term of existence, if such a term is fixed (*see* paragraph 133 above), except if the partnership is not liquidated and none of the partners opposes its indefinite prorogation; (ii) the unanimous consent of the partners; (iii) decision by an absolute majority of the partners, if the entity has an indefinite term of duration; (iv) a case where there is only one partner remaining and such a situation lasts for more than 180 days; and (v) the extinction of the authorization to develop its activities, when necessary. Having seen the general attributes of partnerships, the specific characteristics of each of their most important forms are examined as follows: the simple partnerships, the unlimited partnerships, the limited partnerships, the limited partnerships by shares, and the partnerships upon settlement.

§4. FORMS OF PARTNERSHIP

137. There are different forms of partnerships in Brazil, named Simple Partnerships, Unlimited Partnerships, Limited Partnerships, Limited Partnerships by Shares, and Partnerships upon Settlement, which will be discussed below.

I. Simple Partnerships

138. Simple partnerships were only recently introduced in the Brazilian legal framework through the enactment of the BCC in order to structure non-entrepreneurial activities such as those of an intellectual, artistic, scientific, or literary nature (Article 966, sole paragraph, of the BCC). Their importance lies not in their structure itself but rather in the fact that the provisions contained in the BCC specifically regulating simple partnerships (Articles 997–1033) are also applicable to all types of partnerships when compatible with their specific rules (Article 986) and to limited liability companies, in the latter case unless their articles of association opt for the BCA as a subsidiary source of rules (*see* paragraph 130).

Differing from entrepreneurial companies, the articles of associations must be filed with the Civil Registry of Legal Entities, not with the Commercial Registry. The liability here is also extended to the partner's personal assets in case the partnership's assets are insufficient for the payment of its debts. In view of that, simple partnerships will probably be seldom found, since there are other similar corporate forms that limit liability of the partners.

II. Unlimited Partnerships

139. The unlimited partnership exists when two or more persons (only individuals) assemble to engage in business together under the same designation. That definition alone, however, is not precise enough since it is applicable to any other partnership or corporation. What actually makes the unlimited partnership different is that all of the partners are jointly and severally liable, without limitation, for all obligations undertaken in the partnership's designation by a managing partner, as indicated in the articles of association (Article 1039 of the BCC) (*see* paragraph 133 above). The management will be exercised exclusively by partners appointed in the articles of association (Article 1042 of the BCC).

III. Limited Partnerships

140. The limited partnership is the object of legal treatment in Articles 1045–1051 of the BCC. It is formed both by partners characterized by unlimited liability before third parties for the partnership's obligations and mere contributory partners, whose liability is limited to their capital contribution to the venture.

The personal assets of any and all of the unlimited liability partners may be foreclosed to pay the partnership's debts should the latter's assets be insufficient for that purpose. If there is more than one unlimited partner, they will have the same rights and obligations as the partners of an unlimited partnership.

If the articles of association do not indicate which of the unlimited partners represent and manage the partnership, all of them will be considered to have such powers individually. Additionally, only unlimited partners may lend their names to the limited partnership, which will be designated by the name of all of such partners or of some or one of them, followed by the expression 'and Company' or 'and Co'. Should the limited partner take part in the management of the partnership, he will lose the limited liability status and therefore will be considered to have unlimited liability jointly with the unlimited partners. Whether such an imposition of unlimited liability will be applicable to all of the obligations of the partnership or only to those obligations derived from the limited partner's excessive conduct is not clearly established in the BCC. Therefore, Brazilian legal authors understand that the matter shall be subject to a reasonable examination as to its actual facts. If the undue activity creates a minor obligation for the partnership or is irrelevant to its business and public image, the limited partner who exceeded his/her powers shall be exclusively liable for those specific activities in which he involved the partnership.

However, if the excessive action definitely jeopardizes the partnership's business or even causes a misapprehension of the partner's liability before third parties, the limited partner involved may be held to unlimited liability, jointly with the unlimited partners, for the entirety of the partnership's obligations.

Those rules clearly intend to prevent someone who actually manages the business of a limited partnership from being unreasonably protected under the limited liability status when he has effectively taken part in the management of the partnership.

IV. Limited Partnership by Shares

141. The limited partnership by shares is also a partnership regulated by Articles 280–284 of the BCA and Articles 1090–1092 of the BCC. In this corporate form, the administrators (members of the Board of Directors and Officers) shall necessarily be partners and shall have unlimited liability for the partnership's obligations.

Limited partnerships by shares are regulated by the same rules applicable to corporations (the BCA), except for the provisions pertinent to the Board of Directors (*see* paragraph 76 above), authorized capital, and issuance of subscription bonds (Article 284 of the BCA).

The name of the limited partnership by shares must include only the name or names of the managing stockholders and shall be followed by the expression '*comandita por ações*', meaning 'limited by shares'.

A general shareholders' meeting resolution will depend on the approval of the managing stockholders to be effective in case it decides on any of the following matters: (i) amendment to the by-laws with respect to the partnership's corporate objects; (ii) extension of the term of existence of the partnership; (iii) increase or reduction of the corporate capital; (iv) creation of bonds for participation in the partnership's profits; or (v) approval of the participation of the partnership in a group of companies (*see* paragraph 105 above) (Article 283 of the BCA).

V. Partnership upon Settlement

142. A partnership upon settlement exists when two or more persons, at least one of them carrying on a trade, associate without a separate corporate name for the sake of common profit in one or more commercial transactions, one, some, or all of those persons working in his/her own name in order to achieve the partnership's purposes (Article 991 of the BCC).

Literally, partnership upon settlement would be translated as 'participation account partnership'. That is a partnership wherein the managing partner should account for the results of the partnership's business before the other partners as soon as such results are produced.

The partnership upon settlement is in fact a contractual relationship between two or more persons (individuals or legal entities), which does not result in a separate legal personality or require a separate capital. Because of such characteristics, some Brazilian authors consider that the partnership upon settlement is not actually a partnership or a corporation but rather only a business relationship. The legislation, however, grants partnership status to the partnership upon settlement, and so it shall be treated as such in the present work.

The partnership upon settlement involves a so-called apparent partner and one or more hidden partners. The apparent partner collects the contributions of the hidden partners, eventually mixing them with the apparent partner's own contribution and carries on business activities under the apparent partner's name. He should further distribute the results of such activities to the hidden partners and to himself in accordance with the proportions established in the agreement existing among the parties.

The formation of a partnership upon settlement is not subject to the formalities applied to the other partnerships, as indicated above (Articles 992 and 993 of the BCC). Accordingly, a written agreement is not required, and the filing of any kind of information with any public registry will not be necessary. The apparent partner is the only partner who undertakes obligations before third parties. The hidden partners undertake obligations exclusively and directly with the apparent partner within the limits established by the agreement among the parties.

§5. Taxation

143. As for taxation, any partnerships in Brazil, whether having or not separate legal personality, are basically subject to the same rules applicable to limited liability companies.

Selected Bibliography

Ascarelli, T. Problemas das Sociedades Comerciais e Direito Comparado. 2nd edn. São Paulo: Saraiva, 1969.

Bulgarelli, W. *A Proteção às Minorias na Sociedade Anônima.* São Paulo: Pioneira, 1977.

Carvalhosa, M. *A Nova Lei das Sociedades Anônimas – Seu Modelo Econômico.* 2nd edn. Rio de Janeiro: Paz e Terra, 1977.

Carvalhosa, M. *Comentários a Lei de Sociedades Anônimas.* vol. 1. São Paulo: Saraiva, 1977; vol. 3, 1984; vol. 4, 1978; vol. 5, 1982; vol. 6, 1978.

Comparato, F.K. *Aspectos Jurídicos da Macro-Empresa.* São Paulo: Revista dos Tribunais, 1970.

Comparato, F.K. *Novos Ensaios e Pareceres de Direito Empresarial.* Rio de Janeiro: Forense, 1981.

Comparato, F.K. *O Poder de Controle na Sociedade Anônima.* 3rd edn. Rio de Janeiro: Forense, 1983.

De Leães, L.G.P.B. *Direito do Acionista ao Dividendo.* São Paulo, 1969.

Ferreira, M.G. *Tratado de Direito Comercial.* São Paulo: Saraiva, 1965.

Jurisprudência Brasileira – Sociedade por Ações – vol. 64. Curitiba: Jurua, 1982.

Lopes, M.B. *A Cisão no Direito Societário.* São Paulo: Revista dos Tribunais, 1980.

Martins, F. Sociedades por Cotas no Direito Estrangeiro e Brasileiro. Rio de Janeiro: Forense, 1960.

Mendonça, J.X. *Tratado de Direito Comercial Brasileiro.* Rio de Janeiro: Freitas Bastos, 1934.

Miranda Jr. D.A. Dicionário Jurisprudencial da Sociedade por Quotas de Responsabilidade Limitada. São Paulo: Saraiva, 1988.

Miranda Jr. D.A. Dicionário Jurisprudencial da Sociedade por Ações. São Paulo: Saraiva, 1990.

Moraes, W. *Sociedade Civil Estrita.* Editora Revista dos Tribunais. São Paulo, 1987.

Requião, R. *Curso de Direito Comercial.* São Paulo: Editora Saraiva, 1982.

Peixoto, C.F.C. *As Sociedades por Quotas de Responsabilidade Limitada.* 2nd edn. Rio de Janeiro: Forense, 1958.

Teixeira E.L. & J.A.T. Guerreiro. *Das Sociedades Anônimas no Direito Brasileiro.* São Paulo: Jose Bushatsky, 1979.

Selected Bibliography

Index

The numbers here refer to paragraph numbers.

www.ingramcontent.com/pod-product-compliance
Lightning Source LLC
Chambersburg PA
CBHW071353230926
51846CB00002B/538
9789403520193